GILL: THE LAW OF ARBITRATION

AUSTRALIA
LBC Information Services Sydney
Sydney

CANADA and USA
Carswell
Toronto—Ontario

NEW ZEALAND
Brookers
Auckland

SINGAPORE and MALAYSIA
Sweet & Maxwell Asia
Singapore and Kuala Lumpur

GILL: THE LAW OF ARBITRATION

Fourth Edition

Enid A. Marshall,
M.A., LL.B., Ph.D., Hon. Associate R.I.C.S.,
A.C.I. Arb., F.R.S.A., Solicitor

LONDON
SWEET & MAXWELL
2001

First Edition 1965
Second Edition 1975
Third Edition 1983
Fourth Edition 2001

Published in 2001 by
Sweet & Maxwell Limited of
100 Avenue Road London NW3 3PF.
http://www.sweetandmaxwell.co.uk
Typeset by J&L Composition Ltd,
Filey, North Yorkshire
Printed in Great Britain by MPG Books Ltd,
Bodmin, Cornwall

A CIP catalogue record for this book
is available from the British Library.

ISBN 0421 681 306

No natural forests were destroyed to make this product,
only farmed timber was used and re-planted.

CONTENTS

APPENDICES

PREFACE

This fourth edition of *Gill* is intended, like its predecessors, to be a concise introductory, easily read, text on arbitration, assuming that its readers are students or practitioners new to the subject or requiring a quick revision.

The central topic is, of course, now a new Act—the long-awaited restatement comprising the Arbitration Act 1996. The criticisms of the prior legislation were well-known—three statutes, language inaccessible to the layman, piecemeal amendments, judicial control and the risk to London of a failure to provide a major centre for the arbitration of international commercial disputes.

What we now have is an admirable Act, which no student or practitioner need fear to approach. But you need not take my word for it: just a little dip into *Hansard,* when, with lavish praise, the Bill was passing through Parliament, and you will find numerous passages such as that of Lord Fraser of Carmyllie (*Hansard*, House of Lords, vol. 568, col. 761):

> "[The text of the Act] follows a logical sequence. The language is clear and simple. Above all it is based on the proposition that arbitration is a valid alternative to litigation as a means of resolving those disputes which inevidently arise in trade and business . . .
>
> "The principle of party autonomy is central to the Bill. The parties who are in dispute are able to decide how the arbitration should be conducted. The flexibility and control which this freedom gives to the parties is of critical importance . . . What [the potential users] want is a system which is speedy and cost-effective, is final and fair at the same time."

I express my gratitude to Sweet and Maxwell for their patience and courtesy, and to the writers of those larger works indicated in the "Further Reading" at the end of each chapter.

The law is intended to be stated as at July 10, 2000.

ENID A. MARSHALL.

TABLE OF CASES

TABLE OF STATUTES

[References in **bold** type are to pages where the section is set out in full]

TABLE OF STATUTORY INSTRUMENTS

[References in **bold** type are to pages where the section is set out in full]

CHAPTER 1

THE NATURE OF AN ARBITRATION

GENERALLY

AN arbitration is the reference of a dispute or difference between not less than two persons for determination after hearing both sides in a judicial manner by another person or persons, other than a court of competent jurisdiction.

The person to whom the dispute or difference is referred is called the arbitrator or the arbitral tribunal. The word "tribunal" is used even where there is only one arbitrator.

The parties to the dispute or difference are free to agree on the number of arbitrators to form the arbitral tribunal. There may, for instance, be two arbitrators, one appointed by each side, and in that case there will usually be an additional provision that if the two arbitrators fail to agree the ultimate decision will be taken by an "umpire".

If there is no agreement as to the number of arbitrators, the tribunal consists of a sole arbitrator (Arbitration Act 1996, section 15).

This book is concerned only with commercial arbitrations and not with industrial arbitrations which may be used to resolve disputes in the sphere of industrial relations (*e.g.* arbitrations under the aegis of ACAS).

The Arbitration Acts

Arbitrations are probably as old as legal history itself. The need to have some degree of control exercised by the courts over arbitration was recognised by the English legislature as far back as the Arbitration Act 1697. In later centuries several further Acts were passed culminating in the Common Law Procedure Act 1854. The advent of railways, tramways and other mechanical means of transport from the middle of the nineteenth century led to an enormous increase in the number of arbitrations, and as a result Parliament passed the Arbitration Act 1889, which codified the general law of arbitration as it then stood.

The Act of 1889 and its subsequent amendments, notably the Arbitration Act 1934, were consolidated by the Arbitration Act 1950.

The general provisions as to English arbitration then constituted Part I of the Act of 1950 which was subsequently amended, notably by the Arbitration Act 1979 and the Consumer Arbitration Agreements Act 1988. Part II of the Act of 1950 and the Arbitration Act 1975 concerned international arbitrations under the Geneva and New York Conventions respectively.

The Arbitration Act 1996 is a refreshing new start for the law and practice of arbitration in England and Wales and Northern Ireland. It was passed "to restate and improve the law relating to arbitration pursuant to an arbitration agreement; to make other provision relating to arbitration and arbitration awards; and for connected purposes".

The Act was passed on June 17, 1996 and most of its provisions were brought into force on January 31, 1997 (Arbitration Act 1996 (Commencement No. 1) Order 1996). This date is referred to in the Act as "the appointed day". The sections which were **not** brought into force are sections 85 to 87, which relate to "domestic arbitration agreements", and which would have modified the provisions of the Act in relation to such agreements. The effect of not bringing sections 85 to 87 into force is that the Act applies to both domestic and international arbitrations which are governed by English law.

There are some transitional provisions. In particular "the old law" continues to apply to arbitral **proceedings commenced before** the appointed day (Arbitration Act 1996 (Commencement No. 1) Order 1996). Apart from the transitional provisions, the Act applies to all proceedings commenced on or after January 31, 1997, whatever the date of the arbitration agreement.

The Act wholly repeals Part I of the Arbitration Act 1950, the Arbitration Act 1975, the Arbitration Act 1979 and the Consumer Arbitration Agreements Act 1988. It is not, however an exhaustive code: reference to cases decided before it was passed continues to be appropriate except where changes have been made by legislation.

When passing through Parliament, the Bill, as it then was, won the highest praise for several reasons:

- It sets out a comprehensive and coherent statement of the principles and practice of arbitration in England and Wales and Northern Ireland in a single modern Act.
- It follows a logical sequence.
- Its language is clear and simple, easily understood by laymen.
- "Party autonomy" is central to the Act, *i.e.*, the parties who are in dispute are able to decide how the arbitration should be conducted.
- Another principle central to the Act is "judicial non-intervention", *i.e.*, there is to be no unjustified reference to the courts.
- It enhances the position which London holds as the leading world centre for arbitration.
- It brings the English law closer to the laws of those countries, including Scotland, which have adopted the United Nations Model Law on Commercial Arbitration developed by the United Nations Commission on International Trade Law, commonly known by its acronym "UNCITRAL".

Advantages of Arbitration

There are several advantages, in certain instances, for the parties to a dispute to refer it to arbitration rather than to commence an action in the courts.

The principal advantages are:

(a) When the dispute concerns a technical matter, persons chosen to arbitrate usually possess the appropriate special qualifications.

(b) The process can be speedier than a court case.

(c) There can be a saving in costs.

(d) Unwanted publicity can be avoided.

(e) There is greater flexibility than in court proceedings.

(f) Arbitral awards are, on account in particular of the New York Convention, recognised and enforceable in many more countries than English court judgments.

On the other hand, it should be kept in mind that arbitration does not necessarily result in a more speedy decision than court proceedings: instances abound of arbitrations which have dragged on for years and of actual hearings which have extended over many days; delay may result from challenges to an arbitration agreement or to the choice of an arbitrator; delay is in some cases also caused by the fault of one or both of the parties or their advisers; and there is also the factor that, if the arbitrator is a busy professional person whose services are much in demand, the timetable is more likely to be governed by the arbitrator's availability than by the choice of the parties.

Further, arbitration can sometimes prove more expensive than litigation, since, whereas in a litigation judges are paid and court premises are provided by the state, in an arbitration there will be an arbitrator's fee to pay and possibly also a charge for the accommodation in which the hearing takes place.

The parties do not always regard flexibility as an advantage: in some cases they will prefer all the formalities of court proceedings, with solicitors and counsel employed on both sides.

Arbitrability

A wide range of commercial and financial disputes may be referred to arbitration. However, on grounds of public policy certain matters are not "arbitrable". Obvious instances are crimes and status.

Arrangement of Arbitration Act 1996

The Arbitration Act 1996 has 110 sections divided into four Parts: Part I, the main Part (sections 1 to 84) consists of the general provisions relating to arbitration pursuant to an arbitration agreement; Part II (sections 85 to 98) consists of other provisions relating to arbitration, *i.e.,* domestic arbitration agreements, consumer arbitration agreements, small claims arbitration in the county court, appointment of judges as arbitrators and statutory arbitrations; Part III (sections 99 to 104) relates to the recognition and enforcement of certain foreign awards; and Part IV (sections 105 to 110) has general provisions. There are four Schedules.

Most of this book will be concerned with Part I of the Act. References to sections are to sections of the Act unless otherwise stated.

General Principles

The general principles on which Part I of the Act are founded are stated in section 1:

(a) the object of arbitration is to obtain the fair resolution of disputes by an impartial tribunal without unnecessary delay or expense;

(b) the parties should be free to agree how their disputes are resolved, subject only to such safeguards as are necessary in the public interest;

(c) in matters governed by this Part the court should not intervene except as provided by this Part.

The principle in section 1(b) is referred to as "party autonomy" and that in section 1(c) as "judicial non-intervention".

Mandatory Provisions

The party autonomy provided for in section 1(b) is not limitless; it is stated to be "subject only to such safeguards as are necessary in the public interest".

The Act provides, in section 4, for the division into mandatory and non-mandatory provisions. Mandatory provisions, which are listed in Schedule 1 to the Act, have effect, notwithstanding any agreement to the contrary. Only the other provisions (the non-mandatory provisions) allow the parties to make their own arrangements by agreement. The parties may arrange, for instance, to apply institutional rules (such as those of GAFTA, FOSFA or the Chartered Institute of Arbitrators) or to provide any other means for deciding their dispute.

Schedule 1 lists 21 provisions which are mandatory:

sections 9 to 11 (stay of legal proceedings);

section 12 (power of court to extend agreed time limits);

section 13 (application of Limitations Acts);

section 24 (power of court to remove arbitrator);

section 28 (liability of parties for fees and expenses of arbitrators);

section 29 (immunity of arbitrator);

section 31 (objection to substantive jurisdiction of tribunal);

section 32 (determination of preliminary point of jurisdiction);

section 33 (general duty of tribunal);

section 37(2)	(items to be treated as expenses of arbitrator);
section 40	(general duty of parties);
section 43	(securing the attendance of witnesses);
section 56	(power to withhold award in case of non-payment);
section 60	(effectiveness of agreement for payment of costs in any event);
section 66	(enforcement of award);
section 67 and 68	(challenging the award: substantive jurisdiction and serious irregularity), and sections 70 and 71 (supplementary provisions; effect of order of court) so far as relating to those sections;
section 72	(saving for rights of person who takes no part in proceedings);
section 73	(loss of right to object);
section 74	(immunity of arbitral institutions *etc.*);
section 75	(charge to secure payment of solicitors' costs).

Arbitration and ADR Distinguished

Arbitration aims at the provision of the final decision of a dispute by a private tribunal, and this distinguishes it from several other procedures for the resolution of disputes, referred to collectively as "ADR" (alternative dispute resolution). These include mediation and conciliation, where a third party is involved to assist the parties in a settlement of their dispute, but has no power to impose a final decision on the parties.

Arbitration and Valuation Distinguished

The distinction between arbitration and valuation is more difficult to draw, since each aims at the provision of a final decision by a private tribunal.

The agreement by the parties may make it clear whether an arbitration or a valuation is being contemplated, but the use of words such as "arbitration", "arbitrator", *etc.*, is not conclusive (*Cott U K Ltd v. F E Barber Ltd (1997)*. On the other hand, any ambiguity may be removed by the words used, *e.g.* in *Arenson v. Arenson* (1977), where shares were to be sold at their fair value, and value was to be determined by the auditors of the company, "acting as experts and not as arbitrators", the words explicitly pointed to valuation rather than arbitration.

In arbitration the arbitrator decides on the evidence and applies the law, whereas in a valuation the valuer makes his own inquiries, applies his own expert knowledge, and comes to his own conclusion in accordance with his own expert opinion.

While for arbitration there must be a dispute, present or future, which the parties agree to submit to arbitration (section 6), the purpose of a valuation may be to prevent a dispute from arising.

The main importance of distinguishing between arbitration and valuation lies in the question of immunity from being sued for negligence. The view which had for many years been regarded as settled law was that arbitrators could not be sued for negligence. They had a judicial function to perform and were therefore entitled to the same privilege of immunity from being sued as was unquestionably enjoyed by judges in the courts of law. Valuers, on the other hand, had no such immunity.

The immunity of arbitrators is now stated in section 29 of the Act. An arbitrator is not liable for anything done or omitted in the discharge or purported discharge of his functions as arbitrator unless the act or omission is shown to have been **in bad faith**. An employee or agent of the arbitrator enjoys the same immunity as the arbitrator himself. Further, by section 74, the same immunity is extended to an arbitral or other institution or person designated or requested by the parties to appoint or nominate an arbitrator, and the arbitral or other institution or person making the appointment is not liable for anything done or omitted by the arbitrator or his employees or agents. Again, an employee or agent of an arbitral or other institution or person enjoys the same immunity as the institution or person himself.

All these provisions are mandatory provisions (Schedule 1).

The Seat of Arbitration

English law regards it as essential for an arbitration to have a "seat", *i.e.* a geographical location to which the arbitration is tied and which usually prescribes the procedural law of the arbitration.

"The seat of the arbitration" is defined in section 3 as meaning the juridical seat of the arbitration designated:

(a) by the parties; or

(b) by any arbitral or other institution or person authorised by the parties; or

(c) by the arbitral tribunal if the parties have authorised it to do so.

If there is no designation under (a), (b) or (c), the seat is decided by considering the parties' agreement and all relevant circumstances.

The seat may be different from the geographical location for the hearings. This is especially so in international arbitrations, and some arbitration institutions (*e.g.* LCIA (London Court of International Arbitration) Rules) provide for hearings in different locations.

Stay of Legal Proceedings

Where there is an arbitration agreement and a dispute arises, one of the parties may, disregarding the arbitration agreement, commence court proceedings. The other party may then, under section 9 (a mandatory provision), apply to the court in which the proceedings have been brought to stay the proceedings, so that the matter may be referred to arbitration. Section 9 applies even if the seat of the arbitration is outside England and Wales or Northern Ireland or no seat has been designated or determined (section 2(1)).

The court must grant a stay under section 9 unless it is satisfied that the arbitration agreement is "null and void, inoperative, or incapable of being performed".

An application for a stay may be made even where the matter is to be referred to arbitration only after the exhaustion of other dispute resolution procedures, *e.g.* in a construction contract there may be a provision that the matter is to be referred to the engineer in the first instance and only to arbitration after the engineer's decision.

The party applying for a stay must not have taken any step in the legal proceedings to answer the substantive claim. By taking any such step he is treated as choosing to have the matter dealt with by the court instead of by arbitration. If the court refuses to stay the legal proceedings, any *"Scott v. Avery"* clause included in the arbitration agreement (making an arbitration award a condition precedent to the bringing of legal proceedings) will have no effect.

Limitations of Time

A person seeking to enforce a claim by means of arbitration proceedings may find that if he has delayed too long his right to do so is barred by some limitation of time imposed by statute or by the arbitration agreement.

(1) Limitations imposed by statute

Section 13 of the Act, which is a mandatory provision and derives from the repealed section 34 of the Limitation Act 1980, provides for the application of the Limitation Acts (*i.e.* the Limitation Act 1980, and in the case of foreign law the Foreign Limitation Periods Act 1984): they apply to arbitral proceedings as they apply to legal proceedings.

Most arbitrations would be concerned with the limitation periods applicable to contract or tort. For claims on these grounds, the limitation period is six years from the date of the accrual of the cause of action (which is normally the date of the alleged breach of contract or the date of the damage, respectively).

In determining when a "cause of action accrued", any "*Scott v. Avery*" clause (making an award a condition precedent to legal proceedings) is disregarded.

Section 14 of the Act, which is a non-mandatory provision, is also derived from now repealed provisions in section 34 of the Limitation Act 1980. It deals with the time when arbitral proceedings commence.

In accordance with the general principle of party autonomy, section 14 provides that the parties are free to agree when arbitral proceedings are to be regarded as commenced, and where there is no such agreement, the following provisions apply:

(a) Where the arbitrator is named or designated in the arbitration agreement, arbitral proceedings are commenced when one party serves on the other a notice in writing requiring him to submit the matter to the person named or designated.

(b) Where the arbitrator is to be appointed by the parties, arbitral proceedings are commenced when one party serves on the other party notice in writing requiring him to appoint an arbitrator or to agree to the appointment of an arbitrator.

(c) Where the arbitrator is to be appointed by a person other than a party to the proceedings (*e.g.* an institution such as the ICC), arbitral proceedings are commenced when one party gives notice in writing to *that person* requesting him to make the appointment. (This provision is not derived from the Limitation Act 1980; it should be noted that no notice to the other party to the arbitration is required under this new provision.)

(2) Limitations imposed by the arbitration agreement

There is a mandatory provision in section 12 empowering the court to extend time-limits imposed by the arbitration agreement (or incorporated into the agreement from institutional rules).

The wording may be such as to prevent the claim from being pursued at all, or it may merely prevent the claim from being pursued by arbitration. For instance, a claim would be extinguished if the clause provided that any claim had to be made in writing and the claimant's arbitrator appointed within three months of final discharge of the cargo, failing which "the claim shall be deemed to be waived and absolutely barred" (the Centrocon clause). On the other hand, the contract might limit the time for commencing the arbitration, without extinguishing the claim; the result would be that a claimant who was out of time in relation to his right to arbitrate, might still have a remedy from the court.

By section 12, where an arbitration agreement to refer future disputes to arbitration provides that a claim shall be barred, or the claimant's right extinguished unless the claimant takes within a time fixed by the agreement some step—

(a) to begin arbitral proceedings, or

(b) to begin other dispute resolution procedures which must be exhausted before arbitral proceedings can be begun,

the court may by order extend the time for taking that step.

The section is not limited to commencing arbitration proceedings: it would cover "other dispute resolution proceedings", such as mediation and reference to a panel of experts. This is in line with the increase in use of such alternatives to arbitration.

By section 12, any party to the arbitration agreement may apply for a court order (upon notice to the other parties), but only after a claim has arisen and after exhausting any available arbitral process for obtaining an extension of time.

The predecessor to section 12 was section 27 of the Arbitration Act 1950, but a number of changes have been made. In particular, the previous test of "undue hardship" which would otherwise be caused if an extension were not granted has disappeared and been replaced by two alternative tests: the court shall make an order only if satisfied—

(a) that the circumstances are such as were outside the reasonable contemplation of the parties when they agreed the provision in question, and that it would be just to extend the time, or

(b) that the conduct of one party makes it unjust to hold the other party to the strict terms of the provision in question.

The court may extend the time for such period and on such terms as it thinks fit, and may do so whether or not the time previously fixed (by agreement or by a previous order) has expired.

An extension of time under section 12 does not affect the working of the Limitation Acts. The effect of this provision is that a limitation period affecting a substantive claim will not be enlarged by the grant of an extension under section 12.

The leave of the court is required for any appeal from a decision of the court under section 12. In most cases the decision of the court is likely to be final.

Further Reading

David St. John Sutton, John Kendall and Judith Gill, *Russell on Arbitration*, (21st ed., 1997), Chap. 1 ("Introduction").

Robert Merkin, *Arbitration Law* (with loose-leaf updates), Chaps 1 ("The Framework of Arbitration Law"), 6 ("Breach of the Arbitration Agreement: Stay of Judicial Proceedings"), 11 ("Commencing an Arbitration: Time Limits").

Richard Lord and Simon Salzedo, *Guide to the Arbitration Act 1996* (1996), Introduction and section-by-section annotation.

Bruce Harris, Rowan Planterose and Jonathan Tecks, *The Arbitration Act 1996: A Commentary* (1996), Introduction and section-by-section commentary.

Chapter 2

THE ARBITRATION AGREEMENT

Capacity of Parties

GENERALLY, a person who has a right of which he can dispose is competent to submit to arbitration any questions which affect that right.

As in the general law of contract, there are certain exceptions to the rule that any person or any corporate body can make a binding arbitration agreement.

A minor (*i.e.* by the Family Law Reform Act 1969 an individual under 18 years of age) is bound by an arbitration agreement made by him if it relates to the supply of "necessaries" or to a reasonable contract of service or if it is (or is part of) a contract which is plainly for his benefit; in other cases the arbitration agreement is voidable at the option of the minor but binding on the other party.

The effect of bankruptcy is governed principally by the Insolvency Act 1986.

Where a person, before the commencement of his bankruptcy, has become a party to a contract containing an arbitration agreement, the agreement will not automatically terminate on his bankruptcy, but an option opens to the trustee in bankruptcy to adopt or to disclaim the contract. The position then is, by the Insolvency Act 1986 as amended by Schedule 3 to the Arbitration Act 1996:

(a) If the trustee adopts the contract, the arbitration agreement is enforceable by or against the trustee in relation to matters arising from or connected with the contract.

(b) If the trustee does not adopt the contract and a matter to which the arbitration agreement applies requires to be determined for the purposes of the bankruptcy, then—(i) the trustee with the consent of the creditors" committee or (ii) any other party to the agreement, may apply to the court which has jurisdiction in the bankruptcy proceedings, and the court may, if it thinks fit in all the circumstances of the case, order the matter to be referred to arbitration in accordance with the arbitration agreement.

The position changes once the bankruptcy order has been made: the bankrupt has no longer any power to make agreements affecting his property. The trustee may, with the permission of the court or the creditors' committee, enter into an arbitration agreement concerning outstanding claims against the bankrupt.

Also by the Insolvency Act 1986, where proceedings on a bankruptcy petition are pending or a bankruptcy order has been made, the court is entitled to stay any outstanding proceedings (including arbitration proceedings) against the bankrupt, and these cannot then be pursued against the bankrupt before the discharge of the bankruptcy order except with the consent of the court.

In the case of persons of unsound mind, the court has wide discretionary powers over the patient's affairs under the Mental Health Act 1983, Part III.

As regards corporate bodies the most important category in commercial matters is the company registered under the Companies Acts.

By the Companies Act 1985, as amended by the Companies Act 1989, a party to a transaction with a company (*e.g.* entering into an arbitration with a company) need not enquire as to whether the transaction is permitted by the company's memorandum of association nor need he enquire as to any limitation on the powers of the board of directors. There are two branches to this provision. The first relates to the *capacity of the company*. As to this, the Act, as amended, provides that the validity of an act done by a company (which would include the entering into an arbitration agreement) cannot be called into question on the ground of lack of capacity because of anything contained in the company's memorandum, but it remains the duty of the directors to observe any limitations on their powers flowing from the company's memorandum, and they may be relieved from liability only by a special resolution of the company. The second branch relates to the *powers of the directors to bind the company*. The power of the board of directors to bind the company is deemed to be free of any limitations under the company's constitution provided the other party is dealing with the company "in good faith". Such limitations may derive from a resolution of the company in general meeting or from any agreement between the members of the company. A person is presumed to have acted "in good faith" unless the contrary is proved, and a person is not regarded as having acted in bad faith merely because he knows that an act is beyond the powers of the directors. A member of the company may bring proceedings to restrain the doing of an act which is beyond the powers of the directors, and the directors may be held liable for having exceeded their powers.

If the company comes into financial difficulty the administrator or administrative receiver has, under the Insolvency Act 1986, the power to bring or defend arbitration proceedings. By the same Act, when a winding-up order has been made, no proceedings, including an arbitration, may be brought against the company without the leave of the court, and a winding-up order also causes existing arbitration proceedings to be stayed except with leave of the court.

As regards corporations other than registered companies, the document which constitutes the body may include express provisions affecting the corporation's capacity to enter into an arbitration agreement. If there is no special provision, then the body will have full power to enter into an arbitration agreement.

By section 8 of the Act, unless otherwise agreed by the parties, an arbitration agreement is not discharged by the death of a party, and may be enforced by or against the personal representatives of that party, but this does not affect the operation of any rule of law by which a substantive right or obligation is extinguished by death (*e.g.* an action for defamation).

Agents may enter into arbitration agreements which bind their principals, but the question really turns on the scope of an agent's authority to bind his principal in any particular case. For example in *The City of Calcutta* (1898) there was doubt as to whether the master could bind the shipowners to arbitration. In order to avoid liability for breach of warranty of authority, an agent should ensure that he has the necessary authority to submit the dispute to arbitration. He should also take care to make the submission expressly *as agent*; otherwise he may be held to have bound himself personally.

As a solicitor has implied authority to compromise a claim (*Waugh v. H B Clifford & Sons Ltd* (1982)), he probably has implied authority to bind his client to submit to arbitration.

In the case of a partnership, an agreement for arbitration made by one partner will not be binding on the other partner or partners without their express consent, except in the case where in the carrying on of the business of the partnership it is customary to refer matters to arbitration. However, the other partners may adopt an unauthorised submission by a co-partner; for example in *Thomas v. Atherton* (1878) co-partners were held to have ratified a partner's unauthorised submission of a dispute to arbitration (although, for another reason, the ultimate decision was in favour of the co-partners).

Definition of Arbitration Agreement

Section 6 defines an "arbitration agreement" as an agreement to submit to arbitration present or future disputes (whether they are contractual or not). By section 82, which lists definitions, the term "dispute" includes any difference.

The term "arbitration agreement" therefore covers both:

(a) an agreement to refer an existing dispute to arbitration; in this case the arbitration agreement will often be in the form of a contract separate from the main contract and be referred to as a "submission agreement" or an *ad hoc* submission; and

(b) an arbitration clause included in the main contract, by which the parties agree that *if* a dispute should arise in the future, it will be referred to arbitration.

Section 5 provides that the arbitration agreement must be in writing (but need not be signed by the parties) if it is to be effective under the Act. An oral arbitration agreement (also referred to as a "parol submission") is effective under the common law—a rule of law which is saved by section 81 of the Act—but such an agreement would not be an agreement to which the provisions of Part I of the Act apply. Oral arbitration agreements are, however, rare in modern commercial conditions, especially as the word "writing" is given a wide definition by section 5.

There is an "agreement in writing" by section 5 if:

(a) the agreement is made in writing (whether or not it is signed by the parties);

(b) the agreement is made by exchange of communications in writing; for example in *Frank Fehr & Co v. Kassam Jivraj & Co. Ltd* (1949) there was held by the Court of Appeal to be a "submission" within the meaning of the Arbitration Act 1889 where buyers sent to sellers a contract form with printed terms including an arbitration clause and having attached to it a printed form which was intended to be signed by, but which was not signed by, the sellers;

(c) the agreement is evidenced in writing; an agreement is "evidenced in writing" if it is recorded by one of the parties, or by a third party, with authority of the parties to the agreement;

(d) the parties agree (otherwise than in writing) by reference to terms which are in writing;

(e) there is an exchange of written submissions in arbitral or legal proceedings in which the existence of an agreement otherwise than in writing is alleged by one party and not denied by the other party.

Finally, there is the wide provision that references in Part I of the Act to anything being written or in writing include its being recorded by any means (*e.g.* a sound recording, without the existence of any document).

Because of the requirement for a written *agreement*, the parties must be *ad idem* ("at one").

The Wording of an Arbitration Agreement

An arbitration must be capable of being given a sensible meaning. An illustration of this requisite is *Lovelock Ltd v. Exportles* (1968):

A contract for the sale of timber contained a long arbitration clause in two parts, referring "any dispute and/or claim" to arbitration in England and then a second part referring "any other dispute" to arbitration in Russia.

Held by the Court of Appeal that the arbitration clause was ambiguous and uncertain to the extent of being meaningless, and that therefore the court could not give effect to it and the dispute would have to be decided by the court. The two parts of the clause were inconsistent with one another and it was impossible to reconcile them.

Lord Denning M.R. said: "It is beyond the wit of man—or at any rate beyond my wit—to say which dispute comes within which part of the clause."

The court will, however, attempt to resolve any ambiguity, so as to give effect, wherever possible, to the intention of the parties.

The result is that the court can enforce even an arbitration which may seem to be vague. This particularly arises where the arbitration clause is very briefly expressed.

Some instances may be given of words which have been held to be sufficient to constitute a binding arbitration:

- "arbitration to be settled in London": *Tritonia Shipping Inc v. South Nelson Products Corporation* (1966);

- "arbitration in London—English law to apply": *Swiss Bank Corporation v. Novorissiysk Shipping (The "Petr Schmidt")* (1995);
- "suitable arbitration clause": *Hobbs Padgett & Co. (Reinsurance) Ltd v. J C Kirkland Ltd* (1969); the Court of Appeal held that "suitable arbitration clause" meant that if any dispute arose it would be referred to any arbitration which a reasonable man in this type of business would consider suitable;
- "arbitration, if any, by ICC Rules in London": *Mangistaumunaigaz Oil Production Association v. United Kingdom World Trade Inc* (1995); the words here amounted to a valid and binding arbitration clause, because the clause as a whole read in the context of an international contract for the sale of oil demonstrated that the parties intended to settle any dispute according to the ICC Rules in London, with English law to apply; the words "if any" were to be treated as surplusage or as an abbreviation for "if any dispute arises";
- "any dispute arising from this contract to be settled by arbitration in London in the usual way as soon as it arises": *Naumann v. Edward Nathan & Co. Ltd* (1930); the evidence showed that the dispute had been settled by arbitration in London in the usual way and that the procedure adopted was not contrary to public policy.

Great emphasis is laid on the court's duty to so interpret the words used by the parties as to ascertain, and, if possible, to give effect to the parties" *intention.* An instance is *Shell International Petroleum Co. Ltd v. Coral Oil Co. Ltd* (1999):

The agreement included the following two clauses:

13. "Applicable Law
This Agreement, its interpretation and the relationship of the parties hereto shall be governed and construed in accordance with English law and any dispute under this provision shall be referred to the jurisdiction of the English Courts."

14. "Arbitration
Any dispute which may arise ... in connection with this Agreement shall be finally and exclusively settled by arbitration by three arbitrators in London England in accordance with the rules of the London Court of International Arbitration."

The court's task was to ascertain the intention of the parties. The clauses were not incapable of reconciliation.

If reconciliation is impossible, the court would simply disregard the arbitration clause and in cases of conflict between incorporated arbitration clauses the court would only enforce the most appropriate arbitration clause (*Central Meat Products Company Ltd v. J V McDaniel Ltd* (1952)).

Mutuality

Formerly there was a view that "mutuality" was essential in arbitration, *i.e.* both parties should be bound to refer to arbitration.

This view was especially associated with *Baron v. Sunderland Corporation* (1966), a case arising out of a claim by a school-teacher for additional salary under the Burnham Report. The Court of Appeal held that it was necessary in an arbitration clause for *each* party to agree to refer disputes to arbitration, and that as there was no agreement by the school-teacher in the case in question, there was no mutuality and so the employers were not granted the stay which they sought.

Davies L. J. said:

> "It seems to me that this is about as unlike an arbitration clause as anything one could imagine. It is necessary in an arbitration clause that each party shall agree to refer disputes to arbitration; and it is an essential ingredient of an arbitration clause that either party may, in the event of a dispute arising, refer it, in the provided manner, to arbitration. In other words, the clause must give bilateral rights of reference."

In a learned analysis of the problem in *Union of India v. Bharat Engineering Corporation* (1977) the High Court of Delhi accepted the principle in *Baron* that an arbitration clause giving the contractor an option to refer a dispute to arbitration must be mutual, and decided that a unilateral arbitration clause giving the contractor an option to refer a dispute to arbitration was not an arbitration agreement; and it was only on the exercise of the option that an arbitration agreement arose for the first time.

Baron was followed in *Tote Bookmakers Ltd v. Development & Property Holding Co. Ltd* (1985), which concerned a rent review clause in a lease. This case, however, was overruled by the Court of Appeal in a subsequent rent review case—*Pittalis v. Sherefettin* (1986):

The tenant was a lessee under a 21-year lease which provided that the rent payable before June 24, 1982 was to be £800 per annum and thereafter the annual rent was to be £850 or the open market rent assessed by the landlord. If there was a dispute the rent would be determined by arbitration at the election of the lessee.

Held that an arbitration agreement would be valid if it gave one party alone the right to refer a dispute to arbitration.

There was a fully bilateral agreement constituting a contract to refer, and the fact that the option to refer was exercisable by one of the parties only was irrelevant; there was no lack of mutuality, since the landlord was protected if there was no arbitration, by his own assessment of the open market rent, while the tenant was protected, if dissatisfied with the landlord's assessment, by his right to refer to arbitration.

Baron's case did not truly relate to mutuality in an arbitration clause, but to a clause which was "about as unlike an arbitration clause as anything one could imagine".

Incorporation of Arbitration Agreement from other Contract

Where two or more contracts are closely associated with each other, it is common to find that clauses are incorporated from one contract into the other or others, *e.g.* in the building industry a sub-contract is likely to incorporate terms from the main contract between the employer and the main contractor, in insurance a contract of reinsurance is likely to incorporate terms from the primary insurance, and in shipping a bill of lading issued to a shipper is likely to incorporate terms from the charterparty between the shipowner and the charterer. One of the terms incorporated often is an arbitration clause.

The Act, in section 6, provides that the reference in an agreement to a written form of arbitration clause or to a document containing an arbitration clause constitutes an arbitration agreement *if the reference is such as to make that clause part of the agreement*. The words in italics are not further explained by the Act: one must look at the decided cases to discover when the reference will be such as to make the arbitration clause a part of the agreement.

The incorporation of the arbitration clause may be effected by an express provision in the sub-contract, reinsurance contract, bill of lading or other document as the case may be. However, difficulties arise where there is no express incorporation of the arbitration clause but incorporation of it is left to depend on some general words which are intended to incorporate many other provisions as well.

The preliminary rule to be applied in such cases is that if any of the terms sought to be incorporated conflicts in any way with expressly agreed terms in the sub-contract, reinsurance contract, bill of lading or other document, the expressly agreed terms prevail over the term which would otherwise be incorporated. Normally, it is sufficient for the parties to demonstrate an *intention* to incorporate an arbitration clause by reference to a document which itself contains an arbitration clause, but the rules are more strict in relation to arbitration clauses incorporated from a charterparty into bills of lading: through the cases it has come to be established that general words will not suffice for such incorporation.

An illustration from the building industry is *Modern Buildings Wales Ltd v. Limmer & Trinidad Co. Ltd* (1975). The head contractors for the construction of a building had placed a written order with nominated sub-contractors to supply adequate labour, plant and machinery for the completion of certain ceilings "in full accordance with the appropriate form for nominated sub-contractors". The Court of Appeal held that the words "in full accordance" were wide enough to import the arbitration clause from the main contract into the contract between the head contractors and the nominated sub-contractors, and so the latter were entitled to an order under section 4 of the Act of 1950 staying proceedings in an action commenced against them by the head contractors for damages for breach of contract.

On the other hand an arbitration clause incorporated from a main contract into a sub-contract may not be sufficiently wide in scope to cover disputes between the main contractor and the sub-contractor: it may be limited to making the results of an arbitration between the employer and the main contractor binding on the sub-contractor. Such a situation came before the Court of Session in *Goodwins, Jardine & Co. Ltd v. Brand & Son* (1905). The general contractors for the formation of parts of a railway entered into a sub-contract for the execution of the bridge work. The sub-contract provided that the work was to be done according to plans and specifications which formed part of the general contract between the railway company and the general contractors. One of the specifications was an arbitration clause. A dispute arose between the general contractors and the sub-contractors as to payment of a balance of the price for the bridge work, and the sub-contractors brought an action against the general contractors, who pleaded that the claim should be submitted to arbitration. The arbitration clause was held not to have been incorporated into the sub-contract in relation to the rights *inter se* of the general contractors and the sub-contractors: it was incorporated only for the purpose of making the result of any arbitration between the railway company and the general contractors binding on the sub-contractors.

A reinsurance case was *Trygg Hansa Insurance Co. Ltd v. Equitas* (1998). The primary insurance provided for arbitration of any dispute arising between the assured and the insurers. The reinsurance contract took the same structure as the primary insurance: "this policy is to follow the same terms, exclusions, conditions, definitions and settlements as the policy of the primary insurers". An action was brought under the reinsurance, and T. H. applied for a stay under section 9, the question in issue being whether the general words were effective to incorporate the arbitration clause into the reinsurance contract.

Held that the arbitration clause was not incorporated.

With the exception of incorporation of charterparty arbitration clauses into bills of lading, the rule had come to be firmly established by the time of *Trygg* that general words did not suffice to incorporate an arbitration clause unless the parties had a clear intention to effect the incorporation.

As regards incorporation of an arbitration clause from a charterparty into a bill of lading, the courts gave a narrower interpretation of the words used for incorporation. There was a long series of authorities before it was established that where a charterparty contained an arbitration clause providing for arbitration of disputes arising under it, general words in a bill of lading incorporating into it all the terms and conditions of the charterparty were not sufficient to bring the arbitration clause into the bill of lading so as to make its provisions applicable to disputes arising under that document.

The leading case in the long series was *T W Thomas & Co. Ltd v. Portsea Steamship Co. Ltd* (1912): the charterparty arbitration clause referred to "any dispute or claim arising out of any of the conditions of this charter", and in the bill of lading there were two incorporation clauses:

"(a) he or they paying freight for the said goods, with other conditions as per charterparty"; and

"(b) deck load at shipper's risk, and all other terms and conditions and exceptions of charter to be as per charterparty, including negligence clause."

The House of Lords unanimously held that the arbitration clause was not incorporated in the bill of lading: it was directed only at disputes arising out of the charterparty.

Cases in which the courts have followed that leading case include the following:

- *The "Njegos"* (1936): the words "terms, conditions and exceptions of the charterparty, including the negligence clause" did not have the effect of incorporating the arbitration clause;
- *The "Elizabeth H."* (1962): a bill of lading stated: "all the terms whatsoever of this said charter except [freight] apply to and govern the rights of the parties concerned in this shipment; in a

claim against the shipowners by an indorsee of a bill of lading, the shipowners failed to prove that there was an arbitration agreement between the cargo-owners and the shipowners;

- *The "Annefield"* (1971): the Court of Appeal held that, where the words in the bill of lading were "all the terms, conditions and exceptions . . . including the negligence clause", the arbitration clause was not applicable to the dispute under the bill of lading, since an arbitration clause, not being directly germane to the shipment, carriage and delivery of the cargo, could only be incorporated in the bill of lading by specific words, either in the bill of lading or in the charterparty, showing an intention to provide for arbitration;
- *Skips A/S Nordheim v. Syrian Petroleum Co. Ltd (The "Varenna")* (1983): a charterparty provided: "any dispute arising under this charter shall be settled in London by arbitration; all bills of lading issued pursuant to this charter shall incorporate by reference all terms and conditions of this charter including the terms of the arbitration clause"; the Court of Appeal held that the arbitration clause was not incorporated; "terms" and "conditions" in a bill of lading had for years been construed in the restrictive way, *i.e.* as such conditions and exceptions as were appropriate to the carriage and delivery of goods and did not extend to a collateral term such as an arbitration clause;
- *Federal Bulk Carriers Inc. v. C Itol & Co. Ltd (The "Federal Bulker")* (1989): bills of lading included the words "all terms, conditions and exceptions as per charterparty . . . to be considered as fully incorporated . . . as if fully written"; the Court of Appeal held that general language of this kind was not sufficient to incorporate the arbitration clause, and *Thomas* and *The "Annefield"* were applied.

However, more recent cases indicate that the long-established rule, though still good law, will not apply where there is specific mention of the arbitration clause. Some guidance was given in *The Merak* (1965), a decision of the Court of Appeal. The arbitration clause in a charterparty applied to "any dispute arising out of this charter and any bill of lading issued hereunder", and there was a very wide incorporation clause in the bill of lading: "all the terms, conditions, clauses and exceptions including [the arbitration clause] contained in the said charterparty apply to this bill of lading and are deemed to be incorporated herein". The arbitration clause was held to have been incorporated.

Brandon J.'s view in *The "Rena K"* (1979) was that the addition of the words "including the arbitration clause" were conclusive; the parties had *intended* a bill of lading dispute to be referred to arbitration; he would have reached the same conclusion even at the cost of manipulating or adapting the wording of the arbitration clause (which prima facie was apt to cover disputes arising only under the charterparty).

The "Rena K" was applied by the Court of Appeal in *The "Nerano"* (1996): the bill of lading was held to incorporate the arbitration clause where the words were "all terms and conditions, liberties, exceptions and arbitration clause of the charterparty".

Terms of Arbitration Agreement

While it is generally understood that the parties to an arbitration agreement may insert into it such lawful terms as they wish, the terms of such an agreement must be stated with certainty: a purported arbitration agreement will be void if its terms or its existence is uncertain. Matters relating to the appointment of the arbitrators and the conduct of the arbitration should be specified in sufficient detail that no application need be necessary to the court for interpretation of the agreement.

The courts may give a liberal interpretation to a contract which is incomplete but which contains an arbitration clause indicating that the parties intended to provide machinery for the filling of the gaps, *e.g.* in a long-term commodity contract, the parties may not have specified the price or volume for future years but may have left these to be fixed by arbitration (*The Queeensland Electricity Generating Board v. New Hope Collieries Pty Ltd* (1989)).

Historically the parties' freedom to include the terms of their own choice in their arbitration agreement has been restricted by the attitude of the court in seeking to reserve for itself the right to adjudicate upon disputes. There was thus a conflict between two major principles—the principle that parties should be free to contract on whatever terms they chose and the principle that they were not permitted to oust the jurisdiction of the court.

The most famous expression of the latter principle was that of Scrutton L.J. in *Czarnikow v. Roth, Schmidt & Co.* (1922): a contract for the sale of sugar provided that the contract was subject to the rules of the Refined Sugar Association, one of which stated:

> "neither buyer, seller . . . nor any other person . . . shall require, nor shall they apply to the court to require, any arbitrator to state in the form of a special case for the opinion of the court any question of law arising in the reference, but such question of law shall be determined in the arbitration in the manner herein directed."

The buyers applied to the court to set aside the award on the ground that the arbitrators were guilty of misconduct in not affording the buyers an opportunity to apply to the court for a special case; the court held that the rule quoted and the agreement embodying it were contrary to public policy and invalid as involving an ouster of the statutory jurisdiction of the courts under the Arbitration Act 1889 and the award had to be set aside: Scrutton L.J. said:

> [The Courts] "do not allow the agreement of private parties to oust the jurisdiction of the King's courts. Arbitrators, unless expressly otherwise authorized, have to apply the laws of England . . . . There must be no Alsatia in England where the King's writ does not run."

This principle no longer applies. The principles now applicable are those of "party autonomy" and "non-intervention by the court" as expressed in section 1 of the Act: the parties are free to agree how their disputes are resolved, subject to safeguards necessary in the public interest, and the powers of the court to intervene are strictly limited.

Scope of Arbitration Agreement

The question of whether a particular matter is within the scope of the arbitrator's jurisdiction depends on the interpretation of the words used by the parties in their arbitration agreement.

The scope is wide where the words used are "all disputes", "all differences" or "all claims". For an arbitration to exist there must be a dispute. The Act provides in section 82 that "dispute" includes "any difference". The word "claim" does not necessarily mean that there is any dispute.

The scope of the arbitration agreement will depend on the context of the word "dispute": it may be followed by "arising under this contract", "arising out of this contract", "in connection with this contract", "in relation to this contract" and a variety of other words; these phrases can all have a broad meaning.

In *Gunter Henck v. Andre & Cie S. A.* (1970), where the words of an arbitration clause were "all disputes from time to time arising out of or under this contract", Mocatta J. said that the words "arising out of" clearly extended the meaning that would otherwise have been applied to the clause had it been limited to "all disputes arising under this contract".

Other instances of arbitration clauses which have been held to be wide in scope are:

- "any dispute or difference which arises or occurs between the parties in relation to any thing or matter arising out of or under this agreement" (*Government of Gibraltar v. Kenney* (1956));
- "any dispute arising under the execution of this charterparty" (*Astro Venedor Compania Naviera S. A. v. Mabanaft GmbH* (1970));
- "any dispute arising in any way whatsoever out of this bill of lading" (*Ulysses v. Huntingdon* (1990)).

In *Ashville Investments v. Elmer Contractors Ltd* (1988)) the Court of Appeal emphasised that the question whether a dispute between the parties to a contract fell within an agreement to arbitrate was primarily a question of construction of the arbitration clause itself in the circumstances of the particular case: "there is no principle of law that the meaning of certain specific words in one arbitration clause in one contract is immutable and that the same words in another arbitration clause in other circumstances in another contract must be construed in the same way."

Disputes as to tort may be covered by the words used, as they were in the *Ashville* case by the words in the arbitration agreement "any matter or thing of whatsoever nature arising thereunder or in connection therewith". However, the question as to whether tortious, as well as contractual, claims could be referred to arbitration was less certain. All doubt was removed by the words in section 6 of the Act:

> "an 'arbitration agreement' means an agreement to submit to arbitration present or future disputes (whether they are contractual or not)."

It is recommended in recent authorities (*e.g. Russell*, 2–007) that it is best to draft arbitration agreements to cover future, as well as unknown, disputes, in the widest possible terms, the safest formula being that found in *Government of Gibraltar v. Kenney* (see above).

Separability of Arbitration Agreement

The doctrine of separability involves the question of what happens to an arbitration clause if the contract in which it is contained is brought to an end, *e.g.* by repudiation or by frustration. Does the arbitration clause survive or does it also come to an end?

The House of Lords' decision in *Heyman v. Darwins Ltd* (1942) firmly settled the point that an arbitration clause in a contract may be wide enough to cover a dispute as to whether the contract itself has been repudiated or frustrated:

D. Ltd, manufacturers of steel in Sheffield, by a written contract appointed H. to be their sole selling agent in certain territories. The contract contained an arbitration clause providing: "If any dispute shall arise between the parties hereto in respect of this agreement or any of the provisions herein contained or anything arising hereout the same shall be referred for arbitration in accordance with the provisions of the Arbitration Act 1889."

H maintained that D Ltd had repudiated the contract and he brought an action of damages. D. Ltd admitted the existence of the contract but denied that they had repudiated it, and they applied to have the action stayed in order that the matter might be dealt with under the arbitration clause.

Held that the arbitration clause applied.

The language of the arbitration clause in the contract was described by Viscount Simon L. C. as being "as broad as can well be imagined". Questions as to whether the contract had been repudiated or frustrated were within such a clause. The Lord Chancellor also mentioned matters which the clause would not have covered: he said:

> "If the dispute is whether the contract which contains the clause has ever been entered into at all, that issue cannot go to arbitration under the clause, for the party who denies that he has ever entered into the contract is hereby denying that he has ever joined in the submission. Similarly, if one party to the alleged contract is contending that it is void *ab initio* (because, for example, the making of such a contract is illegal), the arbitration clause cannot operate, for on this view the clause itself also is void."

The doctrine of separability has now been more widely expressed in section 7 of the Act:

> "Unless otherwise agreed by the parties, an arbitration agreement which forms or was intended to form part of another agreement (whether or not in writing) shall not be regarded as invalid, non-existent or ineffective because that other agreement is invalid or did not come into existence or has become ineffective, and it shall for that purpose be treated as a distinct agreement."

Further Reading

Russell on Arbitration, Chaps. 2 ("The Arbitration Agreement") and 3 ("Parties and Institutions").

Merkin, Chaps. 2 ("Nature of Arbitration Agreements") and 4 ("Agreements to Arbitrate Future Disputes").

Chapter 3

THE ARBITRAL TRIBUNAL

Generally

THE term "arbitral tribunal" is frequently used in the Arbitration Act 1996 to denote the arbitrator or arbitrators sitting to decide a dispute. There may be only one arbitrator or there may be two or more arbitrators, and a chairman, or, if there has been no agreement as to the decision of the dispute, an umpire. The term "arbitrator", unless the context otherwise requires, includes am umpire (section 82).

Many of the provisions in the Act relating to the arbitral tribunal are non-mandatory provisions, allowing the parties, according to the principle of party-autonomy, freedom to decide as to the appointment, power, etc., of the tribunal. Where the Act specifies that the parties are "free to agree" on a matter, or a provision is stated to apply "unless otherwise agreed by the parties" it should be remembered that in order to come under Part I of the Act the agreement must be in writing, since section 5 provides not only that the arbitration agreement itself must be in writing but also that "any other agreement between the parties as to any matter is effective . . . only if in writing".

The Constitution of the Arbitral Tribunal

By section 15 of the Act the parties are free to agree on the number of arbitrators to form the tribunal and whether there is to be a chairman or umpire. Unless otherwise agreed by the parties, an agreement that the number of arbitrators is to be two, or any other even number, must be understood as requiring the appointment of an additional arbitrator as chairman of the tribunal. This provision as to the appointment of an additional arbitrator is necessary to prevent the deadlock which would otherwise arise if the two arbitrators constituting the tribunal disagreed. If there is no agreement as to the number of arbitrators, the tribunal will consist of a sole arbitrator. Sole arbitrators have been common in English law.

Appointment of Arbitrators

By section 16 the parties are free to agree on the procedure for appointing the arbitrator or arbitrators, including the procedure for appointing any chairman or umpire.

If there is no agreement by the parties on these points, then sections 16 to 22 provide the following rules ("default provisions"):

—If the tribunal is to consist of a sole arbitrator, the parties must jointly appoint the arbitrator not later than 28 days after service of a request in writing by either party to do so.

—If the tribunal is to consist of two arbitrators, each party must appoint one arbitrator not later than 14 days after service of a request in writing by either party to do so.

—If the tribunal is to consist of three arbitrators—

(a) each party must appoint one arbitrator not later than 14 days after service of a request in writing by either party to do so, and
(b) the two arbitrators appointed under (a) *must* immediately appoint a third arbitrator as the chairman of the tribunal.

—If the tribunal is to consist of two arbitrators and an umpire—

(a) [as (a), above], and
(b) the two arbitrators appointed under (a) *may* appoint an umpire at any time after they themselves have been appointed, and *must* do so before any substantive hearing or forthwith if they cannot agree on a matter relating to the arbitration (section 16).

The court may, unless the parties otherwise agree, by order extend any of the time-limits mentioned. An application for such an order may be made by any party to the arbitral proceedings (upon notice to the other parties and to the tribunal) or by the arbitral tribunal (upon notice to the parties). The court's power may be exercised, whether or not the time-limit has already expired, but the court must be satisfied that any other available recourse has first been exhausted *and* that a substantial injustice would be done if the court did not extend the time-limit (section 79).

Section 17 covers the situation (unless the parties otherwise agree) where each of the two parties is to appoint an arbitrator and one party, referred to as "the party in default", refuses to do so within the time specified. The provision is that the other party, having duly appointed his arbitrator, may give notice in writing to the party in default that he proposes to appoint his arbitrator to act as sole arbitrator. If the party in default does not within seven clear days of that notice being given make the required appointment and notify the other party that he has done so, the other party may appoint his arbitrator as sole arbitrator, whose award will be binding on both parties as if he had been appointed as sole arbitrator by agreement. Where a sole arbitrator has been appointed under that procedure, the party in default (upon notice to the appointing party) may apply to court, and the court may set aside the appointment. The leave of the court is required for any appeal from a decision of the court. Unless the parties agree otherwise, the phrase "within seven clear days" means that seven days must intervene between the giving of notice to the party in default and the appointment of the sole arbitrator (section 78). The court has power to extend the time-limit (see section 79, above)

Section 18 relates to the failure of the appointment procedure. The parties are free to agree what is to happen. Section 18 does not apply if an appointment of a sole arbitrator is duly made under section 17, unless that appointment is set aside. Section 18 confers powers on the court where the parties have made no agreement as to what is to happen and where section 17 does not apply. Any party to the arbitration agreement may (upon notice to the other parties) apply to the court to exercise the following powers:

(a) to give directions as to the making of any necessary appointments;

(b) to direct that the tribunal shall be constituted by such appointments (or any one or more of them) as have been made;

(c) to revoke any appointments already made;

(d) to make any necessary appointments itself.

Any appointment made by the court under section 18 has effect as if made by the agreement of the parties. Leave of the court is required for any appeal from the court's decision.

In deciding whether to exercise, and in considering how to exercise, any of its powers, the court must have due regard to any agreement of the parties as to the qualifications required of the arbitrators, *e.g.* membership of specified trade association, or "commercial man" (section 19).

Chairman and Umpire

Sections 20, 21 and 22 relate to the chairman and the umpire. The former English practice was that when two arbitrators appointed a third arbitrator, he became an umpire. This was in contrast with international practice. The provisions of the Act of 1996 are:

—Where the parties have agreed that there is to be a chairman, they are free to agree what his functions are to be in the making of decisions, orders and awards. Where there is no agreement, then decisions, orders and awards must be made by all or a majority of the arbitrators (including the chairman), and if there is neither unanimity nor a majority, the view of the chairman prevails as to any decision, order or award (section 20).

—Where the parties have agreed that there is to be an umpire, they are free to agree what the functions of the umpire are to be, and in particular—

(a) whether he is to attend the proceedings, and
(b) when he is to replace the other arbitrators as the tribunal with power to make decisions, orders and awards.

If there is no agreement by the parties on these points, the provisions of section 21 apply:

- The umpire must attend the proceedings and be supplied with the same documents and other materials as are supplied to the other arbitrators. (This can result in a saving of time and expense.)
- Decisions, orders and awards must be made by the other arbitrators unless and until they cannot agree. On disagreeing they must immediately give notice in writing to the parties and to the umpire, whereupon the umpire must replace them as the tribunal with power to make decisions, orders and awards as if he were sole arbitrator.

- If the arbitrators cannot agree but fail to give notice of that fact, any party to the arbitral proceedings may (upon notice to the other parties and to the tribunal) apply to the court which may order that the umpire shall replace the other arbitrators as the tribunal.
- The leave of the court is required for any appeal from a decision of the court.

Section 22 provides that where the parties agree that there are to be two or more arbitrators with no chairman or umpire, the parties are free to agree how the tribunal is to make decisions, orders and awards, and if there is no such agreement, decisions, orders and awards must be made by a majority of the arbitrators.

Arbitrator/Advocate

The Act makes no provision for the appointment of an arbitrator/advocate. It was a practice, before the Act, that where the tribunal consisted of two arbitrators, with a third person who was to act as an umpire, the arbitrator could become an advocate for the party who appointed him and appear before the umpire in that capacity.

Judge-Arbitrator

By section 93 a judge of the Commercial Court may, if in all the circumstances he thinks fit, accept appointment as a sole arbitrator or as umpire, but must not do so unless the Lord Chief Justice has informed him that, having regard to the state of business in the High Court and the Crown Court, he can be made available. The fees for the services of the judge are taken in the High Court. The provisions of Part I of the Act are modified by Schedule 3 in relation to judge-arbitrators, *e.g.* references in Part I of the Act to "the court" are to be construed in relation to a judge-arbitrator as references to the Court of Appeal. Such appointments are very rare, possibly because of the heavy workload of the Commercial Court.

Revocation of Arbitrator's Authority

The parties are free to agree in what circumstances the authority of an arbitrator may be revoked. Where there is no such agreement, section 23 provides:

- The authority of an arbitrator may not be revoked except (a) by the parties acting jointly, or (b) by an arbitral or other institution or person vested by the parties with powers to revoke.

- Revocation of the authority of an arbitrator by the parties acting jointly must be agreed in writing unless the parties also agree (whether or not in writing) to terminate the arbitration agreement.
- The provisions in this section do not affect the power of the court to revoke an appointment under section 18 (above) or to remove an arbitrator on the grounds specified in section 24 (below).

Power of Court to Remove Arbitrator

Section 24 is a mandatory provision. It provides that a party to arbitral proceedings may (upon notice to the other parties, to the arbitrator concerned and to any other arbitrator) apply to the court to remove an arbitrator on any of the following grounds—

(a) that circumstances exist which give rise to justifiable doubts as to his impartiality;

(b) that he does not possess the qualifications required by the arbitration agreement;

(c) that he is physically or mentally incapable of conducting the proceedings or that there are justifiable doubts as to his capacity to do so;

(d) that he has refused or failed—

(i) properly to conduct the proceedings, or
(ii) to use all reasonable despatch in conducting the proceedings or making an award,

and that substantial injustice has been or will be caused to the applicant.

If there is an arbitral or other institution or person vested by the parties with power to remove an arbitrator, the court must not exercise its power of removal unless satisfied that the applicant has first exhausted any available recourse to that institution or person.

The arbitral tribunal may continue the arbitral proceedings and make an award while an application to the court under this section is pending.

Where the court removes an arbitrator, it may make such order as it thinks fit as to his entitlement (if any) to fees or expenses, or the repayment of any fees or expenses already paid.

The arbitrator concerned is entitled to appear and be heard by the court before it makes any order under this section.

The leave of the court is required for any appeal.

Resignation of Arbitrator

The parties are free to agree with an arbitrator as to the consequences of his resignation as regards—

(a) his entitlement (if any) to fees or expenses, and

(b) any liability incurred by him owing to his resignation.

If there is no agreement, the following provisions of section 25 apply:

- An arbitrator who resigns may (upon notice to the parties) apply to the court—
  (a) to grant him relief from any liability incurred by him owing to his resignation, and
  (b) to make such further order as it thinks fit with respect to his entitlement (if any) to fees or expenses or the repayment of any fees or expenses already paid.
- If the court is satisfied that in all the circumstances it was reasonable for the arbitrator to resign, it may grant such relief as is mentioned in (a), above, on such terms as it thinks fit.

The leave of the court is required for an appeal.

Death of Arbitrator or Person Appointing Him

The authority of an arbitrator is personal and ceases on his death.

Unless otherwise agreed by the parties, the death of the person by whom an arbitrator was appointed does not revoke the arbitrator's authority (section 26); the arbitration agreement may be enforced by or against the personal representatives of the deceased (section 8).

Filling of Vacancy, etc.

Section 27 provides that where an arbitrator ceases to hold office, the parties are free to agree—

(a) whether and if so how the vacancy is to be filled,

(b) whether and if so to what extent the previous proceedings should stand, and

(c) what effect (if any) his ceasing to hold office has on any appointment made by him (alone or jointly).

If there is no agreement, the following provisions apply:

- The provisions of section 16 (procedure for appointment of arbitrators) and 18 (failure of appointment procedure) apply in relation to the filling of the vacancy as in relation to an original appointment.
- The tribunal (when reconstituted) is to determine whether and if so to what extent the previous proceedings should stand. This does not affect any right of a party to challenge those proceedings on any ground which had arisen before the arbitrator ceased to hold office.
- His ceasing to hold office does not affect any appointment by him (alone or jointly) of another arbitrator, in particular any appointment of a chairman or umpire.

Joint and Several Liability for Fees and Expenses

Section 28 is a mandatory provision. It provides that the parties are jointly and severally liable to pay to the arbitrators such reasonable fees and expenses (if any) as are appropriate in the circumstances.

Any party may apply to the court (upon notice to the other parties and to the arbitrators) which may order that the amount of the arbitrators' fees and expenses shall be considered and adjusted by such means and upon such terms as it may direct.

If the application is made after any amount has been paid to the arbitrators by way of fees and expenses, the court may order the repayment of such amount (if any) as is shown to be excessive, but is not to do so unless it is shown that it is reasonable in the circumstances to order repayment.

These provisions are subject to any order of the court under section 24 (order as to fees or expenses where court removes an arbitrator) or under section 25 (order as to fees or expenses where arbitrator resigns).

Section 28 does not affect any liability of a party to any other party to pay the costs of the arbitration (costs are dealt with in sections 59 to 65 of the Act); nor does section 28 affect any contractual right of an arbitrator to his fees or expenses.

The section, however, covers an arbitrator who has ceased to act and an umpire who has not replaced the other arbitrators.

Immunity of Arbitrator

Section 29, relating to immunity of an arbitrator, is a mandatory provision. The section provides that an arbitrator is not liable for anything done or omitted in the discharge (or purported discharge) of his functions as arbitrator unless the act or omission is shown to have been in bad faith. The provision applies to an employee or agent of an arbitrator as it applies to the arbitrator himself, but does not affect any liability incurred by an arbitrator because of his resignation.

The same immunity extends by section 74 to an arbitral or other institution or person designated or requested by the parties to appoint or nominate an arbitrator: the institution or person is not liable for anything done or omitted in discharging the function of appointment or nomination. These provisions apply also to employees and agents of the institution or person.

Two House of Lords' cases in the 1970s, *Sutcliffe v. Thackrah* (1974) and *Arenson v. Arenson* (1977), left open the question of whether arbitrators were entitled to the same privilege of immunity from being sued as was unquestionably enjoyed by judges in the courts of law. Section 29 now removes any doubt on the matter.

Jurisdiction of the Arbitral Tribunal

Sections 30, 31 and 32 relate to the jurisdiction of the arbitral tribunal. They are based on the Model Law. Sections 31 and 32 are mandatory provisions.

Section 30 provides for the competence of the tribunal to rule on its own jurisdiction. It is an enactment for the first time in English law of the internationally recognised doctrine of Kompetenz-Kompetenz. The doctrine had been recognised previously in English cases; *e.g.* in *Christopher Brown Ltd v. Genossenschaft Osterreichischer Waldbesitzer R GmbH* (1954) arbitrators whose jurisdiction was challenged were held entitled to make their own inquiries into the question whether or not they had jurisdiction in order to determine their own course of action

Section 30 provides that, unless otherwise agreed by the parties, the arbitral tribunal may rule on its own substantive jurisdiction, that is, as to—

(a) whether there is a valid arbitration agreement,

(b) whether the tribunal is properly constituted, and

(c) what matters have been submitted to arbitration in accordance with the arbitration agreement.

Any such ruling may be challenged by any available arbitral process of appeal or review or in accordance with Part I of the Act. Provisions in Part I which are relevant are in sections 31 and 32 (see below) and also section 67 (challenging an award as to its substantive jurisdiction) and section 73 (loss of right to object).

Section 31 provides for how the parties and the tribunal deal with an objection to the tribunal's substantive jurisdiction, without making any application to the court:

- An objection that the arbitral tribunal lacks substantive jurisdiction at the outset of the proceedings must be raised by a party not later than the time when he takes the first step in the proceedings to contest the merits of any matter in relation to which he challenges the tribunal's jurisdiction; a party is not precluded from raising such an objection by the fact that he has appointed or participated in the appointment of an arbitrator.
- Any objection during the course of the arbitral proceedings that the arbitral tribunal is exceeding its substantive jurisdiction must be made as soon as possible after the matter is raised.
- The arbitral tribunal may admit an objection later than the times specified above if it considers the delay justified.
- Where an objection is duly taken to the tribunal's substantive jurisdiction and the tribunal has power to rule on its own jurisdiction, it may—

  (a) rule on the matter in an award as to jurisdiction, or
  (b) deal with the objection in its award on the merits.

  If the parties agree which of these courses the tribunal should take, the tribunal must give effect to their agreement.
- Whilst any application is made to the court under section 32, the tribunal may stay proceedings, and must stay proceedings if the parties so agree.

Section 32 deals with the determination by the court of a preliminary point of jurisdiction:

- The court may, on the application of a party (upon notice to the other parties), determine any question as to the substantive jurisdiction of the tribunal.
- A party may lose his right to object by section 73 if he does not make his objection immediately or within the time allowed by the arbitration agreement or the tribunal.

- For an application to be considered it must *either* be made with the agreement in writing of all the other parties to the proceedings *or* be made with the permission of the tribunal and satisfy the court—

  (i) that the determination of the question is likely to produce substantial savings in costs,
  (ii) that the application was made without delay, and
  (iii) that there is good reason why the matter should be decided by the court.

- An application under section 32, unless it is made with the agreement of all the other parties to the proceedings, must state the grounds on which it is said that the matter should be decided by the court.
- Unless otherwise agreed by the parties, the arbitral tribunal may continue the arbitral proceedings and make an award while an application to the court under section 32 is pending.
- Unless the court gives leave, no appeal lies from a decision of the court as to whether the conditions (i) to (iii) above are met.
- No appeal lies from the decision of the court without the leave of the court, and leave is not to be given unless the court considers that the question involves a point of law which is one of general importance or is one which for some other special reason should be considered by the Court of Appeal.

An application to court under section 32 could be appropriate where the parties had agreed that the arbitral tribunal should not have the power to rule on its own substantive jurisdiction (section 5).

Further Reading

Russell on Arbitration, Chap. 4 ("The Tribunal").
Merkin, Chaps. 7 ("The Jurisdiction of Arbitrators"), 8 "The Office of Arbitrators"), 9 ("The Appointment of Arbitrators") and 10 ("Umpires").

Chapter 4

THE ARBITRAL PROCEEDINGS

General Duty of the Tribunal

Section 33, which is a mandatory provision, sets out the general duty of the tribunal. It reflects the general principle stated in section 1 that the object of arbitration is to obtain the fair resolution of disputes by an impartial tribunal without unnecessary delay or expense. In accordance with that general principle, section 33 provides that the tribunal must:

(a) act fairly and impartially as between the parties, giving each party a reasonable opportunity of putting his case and dealing with that of his opponent, and

(b) adopt procedures suitable to the circumstances of the particular case, avoiding unnecessary delay or expense, so as to provide a fair means for the resolution of the matters falling to be determined.

The section continues: the tribunal must comply with that general duty in conducting the arbitral proceedings, in its decisions on matters of procedure and evidence and in the exercise of all other powers conferred on it.

The court has power to remove an arbitrator under section 24 if the circumstances give rise to justifiable doubts as to his impartiality or if he has refused or failed properly to conduct the proceedings or to use all reasonable despatch in conducting the proceedings or making an award, provided that substantial injustice has been or will be caused to the party making the application for the removal.

Further, under section 68 a party to arbitral proceedings may apply to the court challenging an award on the ground of "serious irregularity" affecting the tribunal, the proceedings or the award. One kind of serious irregularity specified in section 68 is failure by the tribunal to comply with section 33, and another kind is failure by the tribunal to conduct the proceedings in accordance with the procedure agreed by the parties (section 34). In both cases the court must consider that the irregularity has caused or will cause substantial injustice to the applicant.

By section 33 it is the duty of the tribunal to give each party a "reasonable opportunity" of putting his case and dealing with that of his opponent. Because of the use of the word "reasonable", it is not open to a party to make lengthy oral submissions or to present any evidence which he wishes. The tribunal is entitled to indicate to the parties those matters on which it particularly wishes to be addressed and those which it considers are relevant to the matter in dispute. If a party fails to adhere to such guidance, the tribunal might make a re-allocation of the hearing time between the parties.

The section requires the tribunal to adopt procedures "suitable to the circumstances of the particular case". The tribunal may choose to follow the adversarial procedure similar to that used in the courts, hearing the arguments from both parties. Alternatively it may follow the inquisitorial procedure similar to Continental practice, with the tribunal taking the initiative in ascertaining the facts and the law. Another common type of procedure is that where the evidence is presented in the form of documents only, often accompanied by a request from the parties for a hearing at which they make oral submissions and call witnesses; arbitrations of this type are common in commodity arbitrations (*e.g.* under the GAFTA and the FOSFA Rules) and some international arbitrations (*e.g.* ICC, LCIA and UNCITRAL Rules). A simple form of inspection of goods to ascertain their quality can be a suitable procedure where the dispute concerns only the quality of goods supplied under a contract.

Procedural and Evidential Matters

Section 34, which is a non-mandatory provision, provides that it is for the tribunal to decide all procedural and evidential matters but this is made "subject to the right of the parties to agree any matter".

As guidance on what are procedural and evidential matters section 34 provides that they *include* the following:

(a) when and where any part of the proceedings is to be held;

(b) the language or languages to be used in the proceedings and whether translations of documents are to be supplied;

(c) whether any and if so what form of written statements of claim and defence are to be used, when these should be supplied and the extent to which such statements can be later amended;

(d) whether any and if so which documents or classes of documents should be disclosed between and produced by the parties and at what stage;

(e) whether any and if so what questions should be put to and answered by the respective parties and when and in what form this should be done;

(f) whether to apply strict rules of evidence (or any other rules) as to the admissibility, relevance or weight of any material (oral, written or other) sought to be tendered on any matters of fact or opinion, and the time, manner and form in which such material should be exchanged and presented;

(g) whether the tribunal should itself take the initiative in ascertaining the facts and the law; and

(h) whether and to what extent there should be oral or written evidence or submissions.

The tribunal may fix the time within which any directions given by it are to be complied with, and may if it thinks fit extend that time, whether or not it has expired.

The use of the word "include" at the start of this list means that the list is non-exhaustive.

By section 40 the parties must do all things necessary for the proper and expeditious conduct of the arbitral proceedings, and this includes complying without delay with any determination of the tribunal as to procedural or evidential matters, or with any order or directions of the tribunal.

Time and Place of Proceedings

The tribunal has a wide discretion to fix the time and place for the proceedings. In doing so it must have in mind especially the need to "act fairly and impartially as between the parties, giving each party a reasonable opportunity of putting his case and dealing with that of his opponent" (section 33).

The parties may make their own agreement about the time and place, but by section 5 any such agreement, as any other agreements between the parties, must be in writing.

It is important to distinguish between the "seat" of the arbitration and the place where the arbitration is to take place. The "seat" is the legal place to which the arbitration agreement is tied, as distinct from the physical location where the arbitration proceedings take place. The "seat" of the arbitration is defined in section 3 as meaning the juridical seat designated by:

(a) the parties to the arbitration agreement, or

(b) any arbitral or other institution or person vested by the parties with the power to make the designation, or

(c) the arbitral tribunal if authorised by the parties.

Where there is no designation under any of these heads, the juridical seat is decided by considering the parties' agreement and all other relevant circumstances. The word "juridical" relates to the procedural law of the arbitration. The parties are free to choose a procedural law which is different from the proper law of the contract and from the proper law of the arbitration agreement.

Although the seat will normally be the place where meetings or hearings take place, the tribunal may choose some other place or places for these, *e.g.* if witnesses come from some place other than the seat of the arbitration.

Languages and Translations

The language to be used in the arbitration proceedings may be important especially in international arbitrations. The language of the contract under which the dispute has arisen must be considered, and if the arbitrators come from different countries, there is a need to find a language known to all of them or alternatively to have translations. If the arbitrators fail to obtain properly authenticated translations of relevant documents, one or more of the parties may suffer injustice, making the award challengeable on the ground of serious irregularity under section 68.

Formal Procedure

Where there are complex issues of law, the tribunal may decide to have a formal procedure similar to that in court proceedings. The claimant would serve points of claim, setting out the facts and matters on which he relies. The respondent would then respond by serving points of defence addressing the allegations made in the points of claim. There may then be points of reply served by the claimant and occasionally further pleadings in response.

Where issues are less complex, the tribunal may choose the statement of case procedure, consisting of a statement of case, followed by a statement of defence setting out the response. It may take the form merely of short letters from each of the parties, but usually there will be written submissions composed either by the parties or by their legal advisers. The procedure is suitable where the tribunal is experienced and does not need the assistance which pleadings similar to those of court proceedings would provide.

In other situations, the issues may be defined orally or in documents, without further written clarification. Such procedure might be appropriate where the issues were very straightforward or well known to the tribunal.

If amendments are allowed, the parties may amend their written submissions at any time in the course of the reference, but no amendment can, without the agreement of both parties and the tribunal, enlarge the tribunal's jurisdiction.

Disclosure of Documents

The term "discovery" is used in English law to describe the process by which a party to civil proceedings obtains compulsory disclosure of documents and other relevant information from the other party before or during the hearing. Each party is entitled to look at the documents in the other party's list (known as "inspection"). "Privileged" documents are protected from discovery and inspection; examples are confidential communications between lawyer and client for the purpose of advice or evidence in a prospective litigation.

The process of "disclosure" in arbitration is similar to discovery in court proceedings, but, as indicated in (d), above, may in many cases be more limited or even dispensed with altogether, provided that is consistent with the general duty of the tribunal under section 33. The tribunal may order disclosure at any stage of the proceedings, even where it has not made a previous order. Disclosure in arbitration tends to avoid the time-consuming and expensive steps in formal discovery procedures: full lists of documents and inspection are unusual; voluntary disclosure of specified documents or an order from the tribunal for their production may be preferred.

Interrogatories

The term "interrogatories" used in legal proceedings is replaced in the Act by the more familiar terms "questions" and "answers": it is for the tribunal, subject to the agreement of the parties, to decide whether, and if so what, questions should be put to and answered by the two parties, and when and in what form this should be done. This gives the tribunal a discretion as to whether any party is to be examined on oath (or affirmation) or may give unsworn evidence.

Evidence

Under the law prior to the Act of 1996 it was doubtful whether the tribunal had a duty to apply the strict rules of evidence. It was considered that where the tribunal was to consist of "commercial men" there was an implication that strict rules of evidence need not be followed, for "commercial men" would not be familiar with them.

The wide-ranging power conferred on the tribunal (subject to the agreement of the parties) under (f), above, removes all possible doubt. The general duty of the tribunal under section 33, however, must always be kept in mind.

Inquisitorial Procedure

Unless the parties agree otherwise, the tribunal decides whether and to what extent it should itself take the initiative in ascertaining the facts and the law. This authorisation of the "inquisitorial" procedure was not part of English arbitration law until the Act of 1996, but was common in the courts of civil law countries.

Where the tribunal takes the initiative, it must still observe its general duty under section 33 to act fairly and impartially as between the parties, giving each party a reasonable opportunity of putting his case and dealing with that of his opponent.

Oral or Written Evidence or Submissions

The parties may agree that there is to be a hearing, but if there is no such agreement, then it is for the tribunal to decide whether there is to be oral or written evidence or submissions. The tribunal may decide to have a "documents-only" arbitration, which would exclude oral evidence and submissions.

One party alone has no longer a right to insist on a hearing.

Consolidation of Proceedings and Concurrent Hearings

Usually there are two parties only to an arbitration, with the result that an arbitration cannot normally be used to resolve disputes arising under more than one contract.

In some situations it is desirable to have combined arbitration proceedings, with more than two parties involved and concurrent hearings being held of a number of disputes arising from several contracts. Examples are:

(a) the respondent in an arbitration seeks to recover the claim made against him from a third party;

(b) where there is a chain or "string" of contracts and each respondent seeks to pass on liability down along the "string".

To prevent time and expense being spent on the same case several times over with the possibility of inconsistent decisions, the parties may take advantage of section 35.

By section 35 the parties are free to agree that on such terms as may be agreed—

- the arbitral proceedings shall be consolidated with other arbitral proceedings, or
- concurrent hearings shall be held.

The agreement of each party to each contract is required.

The tribunal itself has no power to order consolidation of proceedings or concurrent hearings, unless the parties agree to confer such power on the tribunal.

Legal or other Representation

Unless otherwise agreed by the parties, a party to arbitral proceedings may be represented in the proceedings by a lawyer or other person chosen by him (section 36).

Appointment of Experts, Legal Advisers or Assessors

Unless otherwise agreed by the parties, the tribunal has power by section 37 to appoint experts or legal advisers to report to it and the parties, or to appoint assessors to assist it on technical matters. The more limited role of the assessor, as compared with the role of experts and legal advisers should be noted: the assessor simply assists the tribunal on technical matters, whereas the expert or legal adviser reports to the tribunal and the parties.

The tribunal may allow any expert, legal adviser or assessor to attend the proceedings, and the parties must be given a reasonable opportunity to comment on any information, opinion or advice offered by any of these persons.

It is for the tribunal to reach its own decision on the matter in dispute: it must not delegate the decision to anyone else.

Where the parties wish to bring forward expert evidence to support their respective cases, they should obtain a direction from the tribunal which will define the form in which the experts" evidence is to be given and may limit the number of experts allowed. It is usual for expert evidence to be given in the form of a written report prior to the hearing, and for the expert to be cross-examined on it at the hearing. The experts for the two parties may be directed to exchange their reports and then hold a meeting with the object of identifying issues on which they can agree and thus narrowing the issues to be dealt with at the hearing.

The fees and expenses of an expert, legal adviser or assessor appointed by the tribunal for which the arbitrators are liable are expenses of the arbitrators for the purposes of the Act. This point is a mandatory provision.

General Powers of the Tribunal

Section 38 provides that the parties are free to agree on the powers exercisable by the tribunal for the purposes of and in relation to the proceedings, and specifies certain powers concerning securing costs and evidence which the tribunal may exercise unless otherwise agreed by the parties.

The tribunal may order a claimant to provide security for the costs of the arbitration. Prior to the Act of 1996 an application had to be made to court, where there was no agreement by the parties, to confer this power on the tribunal. In *Coppe-Lavalin NA/NV v. Ken-Ren Chemicals and Fertilizers Ltd in Liquidation* (1994) the House of Lords had held that the court had power to order security even in an international arbitration under institutional rules where the only connection of the parties or the dispute to England was that the parties had agreed to arbitrate in England.

The tribunal's power must not be exercised on the ground that the claimant is—

(a) an individual ordinarily resident outside the United Kingdom, or

(b) a corporation or association incorporated or formed under the law of a country outside the United Kingdom, or whose central management and control is exercised outside the United Kingdom.

Section 38 also provides that the tribunal may give directions concerning property which is the subject of the proceedings or as to which any question arises in the proceedings. The property must be owned by or be in the possession of a party to the proceedings (not a third party). The directions may be for the inspection, photographing, preservation, custody or detention of the property by the tribunal or by an expert or by a party, or they may be for ordering that samples be taken from, or any observation be made of or experiment conducted upon, the property.

The tribunal may direct that a party or witness be examined on oath or affirmation, and may administer any necessary oath or take any necessary affirmation.

The tribunal may give directions to a party for the preservation for the purposes of the proceedings of any evidence in his custody or control. It might, for instance, order a party to keep documents relating to the formation of the contract which might otherwise have been destroyed.

Power to Make Provisional Awards

Section 39 provides that the parties are free to agree that the tribunal is to have power to order on a provisional basis any relief which it would have power to grant in a final award. It can be desirable for the parties to make such an agreement where a large sum may be awarded at an early stage in the proceedings and in trades and industries where cash flow is important, *e.g.* in the shipping trade where it may be appropriate for the tribunal to have power to order interim payment of freight or to order sale of cargo before the final award is made.

In section 39 the instances given are:

(a) a provisional order for the payment of money or the transfer of property as between the parties; and

(b) an order to make an interim payment on account of the costs of the arbitration.

Any provisional order is subject to the tribunal's final decision, and so the final award, on the merits and as to costs, must take account of any provisional order.

The tribunal has no power to make provisional awards unless the parties agree to confer such a power on the tribunal.

This provision was new in the Act of 1996.

The making of provisional awards must be distinguished from the making of awards on different issues: section 47 provides that unless otherwise agreed by the parties, the tribunal may make more than one award at different times on different aspects of the matters in dispute, and an award under section 47 may relate to an issue affecting the whole claim or to a part only of the claims. In the Arbitration Act 1950 such awards were referred to as "interim" awards, but this term is not used in the Act of 1996.

General Duty of Parties

By section 40, which is a mandatory provision, the parties must do all things necessary for the proper and expeditious conduct of the arbitral proceedings, including:

(a) complying without delay with any determination of the tribunal as to procedural or evidential matters, or with any order or directions of the tribunal, and

(b) where appropriate, taking without delay any necessary steps to obtain a decision of the court on a preliminary question of jurisdiction (see page 36, above, on section 32) or law (see page 51 below, on section 45).

Powers of Tribunal in Case of Party's Default

Section 41 provides that the parties are free to agree on the powers of the tribunal in case of a party's failure to do something necessary for the proper and expeditious conduct of the arbitration. The section then proceeds to state three categories of default provisions which are to apply unless otherwise agreed by the parties.

First, if the tribunal is satisfied that there has been inordinate and inexcusable delay on the part of the claimant in pursuing his claim and that the delay—

(a) gives rise, or is likely to give rise, to a substantial risk that it is not possible to have a fair resolution of the issues in that claim, or

(b) has caused, or is likely to cause, serious prejudice to the respondent, the tribunal may make an award dismissing the claim. Formerly, this ground of dismissing the claim was stated to be "for want of prosecution".

Secondly, if, without showing sufficient cause, a party—

(a) fails to attend or be represented at an oral hearing of which due notice was given, or

(b) where matters are to be dealt with in writing, fails after due notice to submit written evidence or make written submissions,

the tribunal may continue the proceedings in the absence of that party or without any written evidence or submissions on his behalf, and may make an award on the basis of the evidence before it. The tribunal is said in such a situation to be acting "*ex parte*" (literally "without a party").

Thirdly, there are in section 41 provisions empowering the tribunal to make "peremptory" orders. If without showing sufficient cause a party fails to comply with any order or directions of the tribunal, the tribunal may make a peremptory order to the same effect, prescribing such time for compliance with it as the tribunal considers appropriate. If the claimant fails to comply with a peremptory order to provide security for costs, the tribunal may make an award dismissing his claim. In the case of failure to comply with any other kind of peremptory order, the tribunal may do any of the following—

(a) direct that the party in default is not to be entitled to rely upon any allegation or material which was the subject-matter of the order;

(b) draw such adverse inferences from the non-compliance as the circumstances justify;

(c) proceed to an award on the basis of such materials as have been properly provided to it;

(d) make such order as it thinks fit as to the payment of costs of the arbitration incurred as a result of the non-compliance.

Where a party fails to comply with a peremptory order made by the tribunal, then, unless otherwise agreed by the parties, an application may be made to the court under section 42 for the court to make an order requiring compliance with the peremptory order made by the tribunal. An application for such an order may be made—

(a) by the tribunal (upon notice to the parties),

(b) by a party with the permission of the tribunal (and upon notice to the other parties), or

(c) where the parties have agreed that the powers of the court under section 42 should be available.

The court must not act unless it is satisfied that the applicant has exhausted any available arbitral process in respect of failure to comply with the tribunal's order. The court must also be satisfied that the person to whom the tribunal's order was directed has failed to comply with it within the time prescribed in the order or, if no time was prescribed, within a reasonable time. The leave of the court is required for any appeal from a decision of the court under section 42.

Securing the Attendance of Witnesses

A tribunal does not itself have the power to require the attendance of a witness, but section 43 provides that a party to arbitral proceedings may use the same court procedures as are available in relation to legal proceedings to secure the attendance before the tribunal of a witness in order to give oral testimony or to produce documents or other material evidence.

This is a mandatory provision, but it is subject to certain limitations:

(a) The permission of the tribunal or the agreement of the other parties is required.

(b) The witness must be in the United Kingdom. If the witness is abroad, an application will be required to be made under section 44, below (court powers exercisable in support of arbitral proceedings).

(c) The arbitral proceedings must be conducted in England and Wales or Northern Ireland.

(d) A person cannot be compelled to produce any document or other material evidence which he could not be compelled to produce in legal proceedings; this protects the witness's right to refuse to produce "privileged" documents.

By section 2 the powers conferred by sections 43 and 44 apply even if the seat of the arbitration is outside England and Wales or Northern Ireland or no seat has been designated or determined, but the court may refuse to exercise any of these powers if in its opinion the fact that the seat is outside England and Wales or Northern

Ireland (or is likely to be so when designated or determined) makes it inappropriate for the court to exercise the power.

Court Powers Exercisable in Support of Arbitral Proceedings

Section 44 confers wide-ranging powers on the court in relation to the preservation of evidence and property. Unlike section 43, however, it is non-mandatory. Unless otherwise agreed by the parties, the court has for the purposes of arbitral proceedings the same power of making orders about a list of matters as it has for the purposes of legal proceedings. If the parties were to exclude these provisions this would weaken the arbitration, but, on the other hand, some desired confidentiality might be lost by an application to the court.

The listed matters are—

(a) the taking of the evidence of witnesses;

(b) the preservation of evidence;

(c) making orders relating to property for inspection, photographing, preservation, custody or detention of the property or ordering that samples be taken from, or any observation be made of or experiment conducted upon, the property; for these purposes the court may authorise any person to enter any premises in the possession or control of a party to the arbitration.

(d) the sale of any goods the subject of the proceedings;

(e) the granting of an interim injunction or the appointment of a receiver.

There are, however, the following restrictions on the availability of section 44, in accordance with the principle of non-intervention by the court:

- If the case is not one of urgency, the court must act only on the application of a party to the arbitral proceedings (upon notice to the other parties and to the tribunal) made with the permission of the tribunal or the agreement in writing of the other parties. It is only if the case is one of urgency that the court may, on the application of a party or proposed party, make such orders as the court thinks necessary for the purpose of preserving evidence or assets.
- The court can act only if or to the extent that the arbitral tribunal (or any arbitral or other institution or person vested by the

parties with power in that connection) has no power or is unable for the time being to act effectively.

- If the court so orders, an order made under the section ceases to have effect in whole or in part on the order of the tribunal or arbitral or other institution or person having the power to act in relation to the subject-matter of the order.
- The powers listed in section 44 apply even if the seat of the arbitration is outside England and Wales or Northern Ireland or no seat has been designated or determined, but the court may refuse to exercise any of these powers if, in its opinion, the fact that the seat is, or is likely to be when designated or determined, outside England and Wales or Northern Ireland makes it inappropriate for it to exercise the power (section 2).

The leave of the court is required for any appeal from a decision of the court under section 44.

Determination of a Preliminary Point of law

Section 45 provides that, unless otherwise agreed by the parties, the court may on the application of a party to arbitral proceedings (upon notice to the other parties) determine any question of law arising in the course of the proceedings which the court is satisfied substantially affects the rights of one or more of the parties.

Examples of questions of law to which section 45 applies are the interpretation of the Arbitration Act 1996 or of the arbitration agreement and the admissibility of evidence. By way of contrast, where the tribunal has a discretion, for instance to make an order, an application under section 45 would not be appropriate.

The section had its origins in the Act of 1979, but some amendment has been made. The predecessor of the section was described by Donaldson L.J. in *Babanaft International Co. S.A. v. Avant Petroleum Inc., "The Oltenia"* (1982) as being "essentially a speedy procedure designed to interrupt the arbitration to the minimum possible extent" and as being "an exception to the general rule that the courts do not intervene in the course of an arbitration". The exceptional case which Donaldson L.J. had in mind was where the preliminary question of law, if rightly decided, determined the whole dispute between the parties.

An agreement to dispense with reasons for the tribunal's award is considered as an agreement to exclude the court's jurisdiction under the section.

An application under the section must be either—

(a) made with the agreement of all the other parties to the proceedings, or

(b) made with the permission of the tribunal and the court is satisfied (i) that the determination of the question is likely to produce substantial savings in costs, and (ii) that the application was made without delay.

The application must identify the question of law to be determined and, unless it is made with the agreement of all the other parties to the proceedings, must state the grounds on which it is said that the question should be decided by the court.

Unless otherwise agreed by the parties, the arbitral tribunal may continue the arbitral proceedings and make an award while an application to the court is pending.

Unless the court gives leave, no appeal lies from a decision of the court as to whether the conditions in (a) and (b), above, are met.

The decision of the court on the question of law is treated as a judgment of the court for the purposes of an appeal, but no appeal lies without the leave of the court, and leave is not to be given unless the court considers that the question is one of general importance, or is one which for some other special reason should be considered by the Court of Appeal.

Further Reading

Further Reading: *Russell on Arbitration*, Chaps. 5 ("Conduct of the Reference") and 7 ("The Role of the Court before and during the Arbitration").

Merkin, Chaps. 12 ("Arbitration Proceedings"), 13 ("Evidence in Arbitrations") and 14 ("Delay and Lack of Co-operation by the Parties to the Arbitration").

CHAPTER 5

THE AWARD

THE MEANING OF "AWARD"

THE Act of 1996 does not give a statutory definition of an "award". The word means the final determination of the issue or claim made by the tribunal in an arbitration.

Once the tribunal has made its award, it is said to be "*functus*", an abridgement of "*functus officio*" (literally "having performed its duty"): this means that the tribunal's authority to act is, as a general rule, at an end.

Section 58 of the Act provides that, unless otherwise agreed by the parties, an award made by the tribunal is final and binding both on the parties and on any persons claiming through or under them, but this does not affect the right of a person to challenge the award "by any available arbitral process of appeal or review or in accordance with the provisions of this Part [of the Act]" There are the following exceptions to the general rule:

(a) Under section 57 the parties are free to agree on the powers of the tribunal to correct an award or make an additional award.

(b) Under section 68 a party to arbitral proceedings may, if there is shown to be serious irregularity affecting the award, apply to the court and the court may remit the award to the tribunal for reconsideration.

(c) Under section 69, unless otherwise agreed by the parties, a party to arbitral proceedings has a limited right of appeal to the court and on such an appeal the court may by order remit the award to the tribunal for reconsideration.

Types of Award

Apart from the final award, it is possible to have the following types of award:

(a) a **provisional** award under section 39, by which the parties are free to agree that the tribunal will have power to order on a provisional basis any relief which it would have power to grant in a final award, including a provisional order for the payment of money or the transfer of property or an order to make an interim payment on account of the costs of the arbitration;

(b) a **partial** award under section 47, which permits the tribunal, unless otherwise agreed by the parties, to make more than one award at different times on different aspects of the matters to be decided; the award may, in particular, relate to an issue affecting the whole claim or it may relate to a part only of the claims or cross-claims submitted to the tribunal; if the tribunal makes a partial award, it must specify in the award the issue or claim or part of a claim which is the subject-matter of the award;

(c) an **agreed** award under section 51, if during the arbitral proceedings the parties settle the dispute; the tribunal must then terminate the substantive proceedings, and if the parties request an agreed award and the tribunal does not object to doing so, the tribunal must issue an agreed award; if the tribunal does object, the parties cannot compel the tribunal to issue an agreed award; an agreed award must state that it is **an award of the tribunal** (not necessarily an agreed award), and the provisions as to awards in sections 52 to 58 (see below) and as to costs of the arbitration in sections 59 to 65 (see below) apply to it;

(d) a **reasoned** award under section 52, which provides that the award must contain the reasons for the award unless it is an agreed award or the parties have agreed to dispense with reasons; an agreement to dispense with reasons has, by section 69, the effect of excluding the court's jurisdiction for an appeal to the court on a question of law arising out of the award;

(d) an **additional** award under section 57, by which the tribunal, on its own initiative or on the application of a party, may make an additional award in respect of any claim which was presented to the tribunal but was not dealt with in the award; and

(e) a **draft** award, which is not properly an award and will not be binding on the parties until confirmed by the tribunal.

The term "interim award", used in section 14 of the Act of 1950, does not appear in the Act of 1996.

An award must be distinguished from procedural orders and directions (see on section 34 (page 40), above): such orders and directions are not awards.

Remedies Available to the Tribunal

By section 48 the parties are free to agree on the powers which the tribunal may exercise as regards remedies. The section then sets out a non-exhaustive list of the powers which the tribunal has unless otherwise agreed by the parties:

(a) The tribunal may order the payment of a sum of money. The payment may be either as a debt or by way of damages. The order may be to pay in any currency. If the award is in a foreign currency it may be enforced in England by converting it to sterling at the rate of exchange ruling at the date of the award (*Jugoslavenska Oceanska Plovidba v. Castle Investment Co. Inc. (The Kozara)* (1974)). The tribunal should make the award in the proper currency of the contract under which the dispute arose unless the parties have agreed otherwise. If there is no other indication of what the proper currency is, it is that which best expresses the claimant's loss, *i.e.*, usually the currency of the claimant's business (*Services Europe Atlantique Sud (SEAS) v. Stockholms Rederiaktiebolag Svea (The Despina R, The Folias,* 1979).

(b) The tribunal may make a declaration as to any matter to be determined in the proceedings. The wording "any matter to be determined in the proceedings" implies that a wide interpretation is to be given to the provision. This declaratory remedy would be appropriate, for instance, where the parties wanted a decision as to the existence or meaning of a contract or a decision on their rights, but would not cover academic or hypothetical questions or claims which have not actually been made.

(c) The tribunal has the same powers as the court:

(i) to order a party to do or refrain from doing anything ("injunctive relief"); where there is urgency to protect evidence or property, it is usually preferable to apply to the court under section 44 for an interim injunction; where there is no urgency, the parties should first apply to the tribunal instead of to the court;

(ii) to order specific performance of a contract (other than a contract relating to land);

(iii) to order the rectification, setting aside or cancellation of a deed or other document; this provision clarifies an area which previously depended on the terms used in the arbitration agreement.

Interest

The provisions of sections 19A and 20 of the Act of 1950 relating to the award of interest on awards have been replaced by section 49 of the Act of 1996.

In accordance with the principle of party autonomy, section 49 provides that the parties are free to agree on the powers of the tribunal on the award of interest, but that unless otherwise agreed by the parties the following provisions of section 49 apply.

First, there is a provision on *pre-award* interest: the tribunal may award simple or compound interest from such dates, at such rates and with such rests as it considers meets the justice of the case—

(a) on the whole or part of any amount awarded by the tribunal, in respect of any period up to the date of the award;

(b) on the whole or part of any amount claimed in the arbitration and outstanding at the commencement of the arbitral proceedings but paid before the award was made, in respect of any period up to the date of payment.

In contrast to section 19A of the Act of 1950, which conferred on an arbitrator a discretion to award only simple interest, section 49 of the Act of 1996 permits the tribunal to award either simple or compound interest, the latter being regarded as a compensatory amount.

The amount on which interest is payable is either (a) the amount awarded (or part of it) or (b) the amount (or part of it) claimed in the arbitration and outstanding at the commencement of the arbitral proceedings but paid before the award was made. The period for the cessation of the running of the interest is, under (a), the date of the award, and under (b) the date of payment (though the award has not yet been made).

As regards *post-award* interest, section 49 provides that the tribunal may award simple or compound interest from the date of the award (or any later date) until payment, at such rates and with such rests as it considers meets the justice of the case, on the outstanding amount of any award (including any pre-award interest and any award as to costs).

The provisions of section 49 do not affect any other power of the tribunal to award interest, for instance where institutional rules provide for a power to award interest, as the LCIA Rules do.

Extension of Time for Making an Award

Section 50 deals with the court's power to extend the agreed time limit for making an award.

The parties or institutional rules (*e.g.* the ICC Rules which require the award to be made within six months from the signing of the terms of reference) often impose a time limit for the making of the award.

Unlike section 12, relating to the power of the court to extend the time for beginning arbitral proceedings, which is a mandatory provision (see above, page 9), section 50 is a non-mandatory provision.

It provides that, unless otherwise agreed by the parties, where there is a time limit for the making of an award, then the court may by order extend the time. An application for an order may be made by:

(a) the tribunal, upon notice to the parties; or

(b) any party to the proceedings, upon notice to the tribunal and the other parties.

In each case the application can be made only after exhausting any available arbitral process for obtaining an extension of time (*e.g.* under institutional rules).

The court can only make an order if satisfied that a substantial injustice would otherwise be done.

In other respects the court has full discretion: it may extend the time for such period and on such terms as it thinks fit, and may do so whether or not the time previously fixed (by the agreement or by a previous order) has expired.

The leave of the court is required for any appeal from a decision of the court under section 50.

Formal Requirements of an Award

Sections 52 to 56 consist of a number of provisions relating to the procedure for the making and delivery of an award. Apart from section 56 (power to withhold award in case of non-payment), which is mandatory, the provisions are non-mandatory.

The parties are free to agree on the form of an award (*e.g.* they may agree that the award is to be parol (oral), but this would be rare).

Section 52 provides that in the absence of any agreement by the parties:

(a) The award must be in writing signed by all the arbitrators *or* all those assenting to the award; this gives dissenting arbitrators the right not to sign the award, but if the arbitration agreement requires all the arbitrators to sign the award, a dissenting arbitrator would be in breach of duty if he refused to sign (*Cargill International S.A. v. Sociedad Iberica de Moluracion S.A.* (1998)); the arbitrators need not all sign at the same place or time.

(b) The award must contain the reasons for the award unless it is an agreed award or the parties have agreed to dispense with reasons.

(c) The award must state the seat of the arbitration; by section 53, unless otherwise agreed by the parties, where the seat of the arbitration is in England and Wales or Northern Ireland, any award in the proceedings is to be treated as made there, regardless of where it was signed, despatched or delivered to any of the parties; the provisions of the Act which will apply depend on the seat; by section 2 the provisions of Part I of the Act apply where the seat of the arbitration is in England and Wales or Northern Ireland but certain sections (sections 9 to 11 on stay of legal proceedings, etc. section 66 on enforcement of arbitral awards and (where not inappropriate) section 43 on securing the attendance of witnesses and section 44 on court powers in support of arbitral proceedings apply even if the seat is outside England and Wales or Northern Ireland or no seat has been designated; also by section 2 the court may exercise a power conferred by any other provision of Part I to support the arbitral process where, though no seat has been designated, the court is satisfied that, because of a connection with England and Wales or Northern Ireland, it would be appropriate to exercise the power.

(d) The award must state the date when it was made; the date is necessary, for instance, for the calculation of interest due on the award, for deciding whether the award has been made within any agreed time limit, and by section 70 to comply with the requirement that an application or appeal must be brought within 28 days of the date of the award; by section 54, unless otherwise agreed by the parties, the tribunal may decide what is to be taken to be the date on which the award was made, and in the absence of any such decision, the date of the award is to be taken to be the date on which it was signed by the arbitrator, or, where more than one arbitrator has signed the award, by the last of them.

Section 55 provides that the parties are free to agree on the requirements for the notification of the award to the parties, but if there is no such agreement, the award must be notified to all the parties by service on them of copies of the award, and this must be done without delay after the award is made. Notification to the parties (also sometimes referred to as "notification and publication") must be distinguished from delivery. The tribunal has power under section 56 to withhold delivery of the award for non-payment of fees and expenses, and nothing in section 55 affects the mandatory provisions in section 56.

The tribunal, by section 56, may refuse to deliver an award to the parties except upon full payment of the fees and expenses of the arbitrators. However, if the tribunal refuses on that ground to deliver an award, a party to the arbitral proceedings may (upon notice to the other parties and the tribunal) apply to the court, which may order that:

(a) the tribunal shall deliver the award on the payment into court by the applicant of the fees and expenses demanded, or such lesser amount as the court may specify,

(b) the amount of the fees and expenses properly payable shall be determined by such means and upon such terms as the court may direct, and

(c) out of the money paid into court there shall be paid out such fees and expenses as may be found to be properly payable and the balance of the money (if any) shall be paid out to the applicant.

An application to the court cannot be made where there is any available arbitral process for appeal or review of the amount of the fees or expenses demanded.

The provisions of section 56 apply not only to the tribunal but also to any arbitral or other institution or person vested by the parties with powers in relation to the delivery of the tribunal's award, and in that case the references to the fees and expenses of the arbitrators include the fees and expenses of that institution or person.

The leave of the court is required for any appeal from a decision of the court under section 56.

Correction of Award or Additional Award

Section 57 provides that the parties are free to agree on the powers of the tribunal to correct an award or make an additional award, but insofar as there is no such agreement, the following provisions of section 57 apply: the tribunal may on its own initiative or on the application of a party:

(a) correct an award so as to remove any clerical mistake or error arising from an accidental slip or omission or clarify or remove any ambiguity in the award; or

(b) make an additional award in respect of any claim (including a claim for interest or costs) which was presented to the tribunal but was not dealt with in the award.

These powers must not be exercised without the other parties being first given a reasonable opportunity to make representations to the tribunal.

Part (a), above, is often referred to as "the slip rule". It comprised section 17 of the Act of 1950 ("Power to correct slips"), but without any reference to the removal of an ambiguity.

An *application* for the exercise of the powers in section 57 must be made within 28 days of the date of the award or such longer period as the parties may agree.

Any *correction* of an award must be made within 28 days of the date the application was received by the tribunal or, where the correction is made by the tribunal on its own initiative, within 28 days of the date of the award or, in either case, such longer period as the parties may agree. Any correction forms part of the award.

An *additional award* must be made within 56 days of the date of the original award or such longer period as the parties may agree.

Further Reading

Russell on Arbitration, Chap. 6 ("The Award").
Merkin, Chap. 16 ("Arbitration Awards").

CHAPTER 6

COSTS

THE MEANING OF COSTS

PRIOR to the Act of 1996 a distinction was drawn between "costs of the reference" and "costs of the award". The terminology has been replaced and clarified by sections 59 to 65 of the Act of 1996. In these sections the term "costs of the arbitration" denotes:

(a) the arbitrators' fees and expenses; these include any fees and expenses of an arbitrator removed by the court if the court considers him entitled to fees or expenses (s. 24) and to any fees and expenses of an arbitrator who has resigned and who has, in the absence of any agreement between the arbitrator and the parties, applied to the court to make such an order as it thinks fit with respect to entitlement to fees or expenses (s. 25); "arbitrator" in this context includes an umpire (s. 82) who has sat in on the proceedings, though he has not yet been called on to decide the dispute;

(b) the fees and expenses of any arbitral institution concerned, *e.g.* an arbitral institution which has appointed the arbitrators;

(c) the legal or other costs of the parties, including the costs incurred in negotiating the reference to the arbitrators;

(d) any costs incidental to any proceedings to determine the amount of the recoverable costs of the arbitration; there is a cross-reference here to section 63 which relates to the recoverable costs; under section 63 an application may be made to the court for the determination of the recoverable costs; the costs of such proceedings would be included under (d).

Award of Costs

By section 61 the tribunal may make an award allocating the costs of the arbitration as between the parties, but this is subject to any agreement of the parties.

Section 61 also provides that unless the parties otherwise agree, the tribunal must award costs on the general principle that costs should follow the event except where it appears to the tribunal that in the circumstances this is not appropriate in relation to the whole or part of the costs. The effect of costs following the event is that the successful party is awarded his costs.

There are, however, two restrictions on the agreement which the parties may make as to the costs:

- section 60 provides that an agreement which has the effect that a party is to pay the whole or part of the costs of the arbitration in any event is only valid if made after the dispute in question has arisen; this is a mandatory provision; and
- section 62 provides that unless the parties otherwise agree, any obligation under an agreement between them as to how the costs are to be borne, or under an award allocating the costs of the arbitration, extends only to such costs as are "recoverable"; the question of which costs are "recoverable" is decided in accordance with section 63.

Recoverable Costs of the Arbitration

By section 63 the parties are free to agree what costs of the arbitration are "recoverable", and insofar as there is no such agreement, the following provisions of section 63 apply:

(a) The tribunal may determine by award the recoverable costs of the arbitration on such basis as it thinks fit, and if it does so, it must specify (i) the basis on which it has acted, and (ii) the items of recoverable costs and the amount referable to each; this latter requirement means that it would not be appropriate for the tribunal to award a lump sum.

(b) If the tribunal does not determine the recoverable costs of the arbitration, any party to the arbitral proceedings may apply to the court (upon notice to the other parties), and the court may then either (i) determine the recoverable costs of the arbitration on such basis as it thinks fit, or (ii) order that they shall be determined by such means and upon such terms as it may specify.

(c) Unless the tribunal or the court determines otherwise, the recoverable costs of the arbitration are to be determined on the basis that there shall be allowed a reasonable amount in respect of all costs reasonably incurred, and any doubt as to whether costs were of a reasonable amount or were reasonably incurred is to be resolved in favour of the paying party.

These provisions of section 63 are subject to section 64 (recoverable fees and expenses of arbitrators); and they do not affect any right of any expert, legal adviser or assessor appointed by the tribunal, or any arbitral institution, to payment of their fees and expenses.

Recoverable Fees and Expenses of Arbitrators

The tribunal's power under section 63, above, to determine the recoverable costs of the arbitration includes the power to determine its own fees and expenses, but section 64 restricts the tribunal's power in this respect by providing that the fees and expenses of the arbitrators are to be only such reasonable fees and expenses as are appropriate in the circumstances and that where there is doubt as to what reasonable fees and expenses are appropriate in the circumstances, an application may be made to the court by any party (upon notice to the other parties) for the court to determine the matter or to order that it be determined by such means and upon such terms as the court may specify.

An order under section 64 is subject to any order made under section 24 or section 25. Under section 24 (power of court to remove arbitrator) where the court removes an arbitrator, it may make such order as it thinks fit with respect to his entitlement (if any) to fees or expenses or their repayment, and similarly under section 25 (resignation of arbitrator) an arbitrator who resigns his appointment may apply to the court for an order as to entitlement to, or repayment of, fees or expenses.

Power to Limit Recoverable Costs

Section 65 consists of a new provision, which confers on the tribunal a power to limit in advance the amount of recoverable costs. The section provides that:

(a) unless otherwise agreed by the parties, the tribunal may direct that the recoverable costs of the arbitration, or of any part of the arbitral proceedings, shall be limited to a specified amount; and

(b) any direction may be made or varied at any stage, but this must be done sufficiently in advance of the incurring of the costs, or the taking of any steps in the proceedings, for the limit to be taken into account.

The intention underlying the provision is to persuade the parties not to incur unnecessary costs by making it clear in advance that costs incurred above the specified amount would not be recoverable even by the successful party.

This new power of the tribunal is in line with the tribunal's general duty under section 33 to adopt procedures suitable to the circumstances, avoiding unnecessary delay or expense.

Sealed Offers

A "sealed" offer is the equivalent in arbitration of payment into court in legal proceedings. It will usually take the form of a letter, the contents of which are not made known to the arbitrator. A time-limit will be imposed for acceptance—commonly 21 days.

The effect of a sealed offer depends on whether the claimant achieves more by rejecting the respondent's offer and going on with the arbitration than he would obtain by accepting the offer. If the claimant, having rejected the sealed offer, fails to obtain more, the tribunal would generally order the claimant to pay both parties' costs from the date specified for acceptance of the sealed offer. On the other hand, if the arbitrator's award is for more than the amount of the sealed offer, the arbitrator may apply the general principle that costs follow the event (*Tramountana Armadora S. A. v. Atlantic Shipping Co. S. A.* (1978)). These rules are not inflexible, but if the arbitrator departs from them, it is advisable for him to state his reasons for doing so.

Further Reading

Russell on Arbitration, Chap. 6 ("The Award").
Merkin, Chap. 16 ("Arbitration Awards").

CHAPTER 7

POWERS OF THE COURT IN RELATION TO AWARD

INTRODUCTION

SECTIONS 66 to 71 come under the main heading of "Powers of the court in relation to award". They deal with three separate topics:

(a) enforcement of the award;

(b) challenging the award; and

(c) appeal on a point of law.

(A) ENFORCEMENT OF THE AWARD

Section 58 provides that, unless otherwise agreed by the parties, an award is final and binding both on the parties and on any persons claiming through or under them. This means that, subject to the contrary agreement of the parties and subject to the right to challenge the award under (b), above, the award is immediately enforceable. The parties may, of course, implement the award voluntarily, but if they do not, then the provisions of section 66 on enforcement become applicable. Section 66 is a mandatory provision.

By section 2 of the Act, section 66 applies even if the seat of the arbitration is outside England and Wales or Northern Ireland or no seat has been designated or determined.

The normal procedure for enforcing an award is the summary procedure under section 66. The provision is that, *by leave of the court*, an award may be enforced in the same manner as a judgment or order of the court to the same effect. The result is that all the methods of enforcing a judgment of the court are available to the party who has applied for, and been granted, leave.

The summary procedure for obtaining leave is straightforward. The application is made "*ex parte*", supported by an affidavit containing a full and frank disclosure of any matter which might affect the granting of leave.

Section 66, however, provides that leave to enforce an award must not be given where the person against whom it is sought to be enforced shows that the tribunal lacked substantive jurisdiction to make the award. That party must raise his objection promptly; otherwise he may lose his right to object, as provided by section 73 (Loss of right to object). "Substantive jurisdiction" is defined in section 82 (Minor definitions) which refers back to section 30. The provision in section 30 is that unless otherwise agreed by the parties, the arbitral tribunal may rule on its own substantive jurisdiction, *i.e.*, as to (i) whether there is a valid arbitration agreement, (ii) whether the tribunal is properly constituted, and (iii) what matters have been submitted to arbitration in accordance with the arbitration agreement.

Apart from the question of substantive jurisdiction, the court has a discretion not to give leave to enforce the award summarily, *e.g.* in exceptional cases it may refuse to give leave where the award is so defective in form or in substance that it is incapable of being enforced or its enforcement would be contrary to public policy.

An alternative to the normal summary procedure for enforcement under section 66, is for the party seeking to enforce the award to bring an action on the award at common law. This right is preserved by section 66. It requires the issue of a writ and proof of the validity of the submission agreement and the award. It would be necessary to use this procedure if the arbitration agreement in respect of which the award has been made does not satisfy the requirements for an arbitration agreement specified in sections 5 and 6 (Agreements to be in writing and Definition of arbitration agreement, respectively). If the particular arbitration agreement, not satisfying sections 5 and 6, contained an implied obligation to perform the award, failure to perform the award would be a breach of the arbitration agreement, and the successful party could then bring an action for the breach and obtain a judgment in terms of the award.

(B) Challenging the Award

There are two categories of challenge. The first, the substantive jurisdiction challenge, is in section 67, and the second, the serious irregularity challenge, is in section 68. There are also supplementary provisions in section 70 which apply to applications both under section 67 and under section 68. Sections 67 and 68 and the supplementary provisions relating to these sections are mandatory provisions. The effect of a court order resulting from a challenge under section 67 or 68 is provided for in section 71, and these provisions are also mandatory. Some consideration is also given below to the mandatory sections 72 and 73 (Saving for rights of person who takes no part in proceedings, and Loss of right to object, respectively), though they come under a different heading ("*Miscellaneous*") in the Act.

First, section 67 provides that a party to arbitral proceedings may (upon notice to the other parties and to the tribunal) apply to the court:

(i) challenging any award of the tribunal as to its substantive jurisdiction; or

(ii) for an order declaring an award made by the tribunal on the merits to be of no effect, in whole or in part, because the tribunal did not have substantive jurisdiction.

The arbitral tribunal may continue the arbitral proceedings and make a further award while an application to the court under section 67 is pending.

On an application under section 67, the court may by order (i) confirm the award, (ii) vary the award, or (iii) set aside the award in whole or in part.

Leave of the court is required for any appeal from a decision of the court under this section.

To these provisions in section 67 there must be added the provisions of sections 70 to 73 insofar as they relate to a challenge under section 67:

- *Section 70* imposes the following mandatory restrictions on an application under section 67:

  (1) An application may not be brought if the applicant has not first exhausted any available arbitral process of appeal or review and any available recourse under section 57 (which deals with the correction of an award or the making of an additional award).

  (2) An application must be brought within 28 days of the date of the award, or, if there has been any arbitral process of appeal or review, of the date when the applicant was notified of the result of that process.

  (3) If it appears to the court that the award does not contain the tribunal's reasons or does not set out its reasons in

sufficient detail to enable the court properly to consider the application, then the court may order the tribunal to state the reasons for its award in sufficient detail for that purpose. Additional costs of the arbitration may result from such an order and the court may make such order as it thinks fit with respect to these additional costs.

(4) The court may order the applicant to provide security for the costs of the application, and may direct that the application be dismissed if the order is not complied with. The power to order security for costs is not to be exercised on the ground that the applicant is an individual ordinarily resident outside the United Kingdom or a corporation or association formed outside the United Kingdom or whose central management and control is exercised outside the United Kingdom.

(5) The court may order that any money payable under the award shall be brought into court or otherwise secured pending the decision of the application, and may direct that the application be dismissed if the order is not complied with.

- *Section 71*, relating to the effect of an order of the court, provides the following mandatory provisions in relation to an application under section 67:

  (1) Where the award is varied, the variation has effect as part of the tribunal's award.

  (2) Where the award is set aside, in whole or in part, the court may also order that any provision that an award is a condition precedent to the bringing of legal proceedings in respect of a matter to which the arbitration agreement applies, is of no effect as regards the subject-matter of the award (or the relevant part of the award), *i.e.* the court may order that a *Scott v. Avery* (1856) clause is to have no effect.

- *Section 72*, a mandatory provision, saves the rights of a person who is alleged to be a party to arbitral proceedings but who takes no part in the proceedings: he has the same right as a party to the arbitral proceedings to challenge an award under section 67 on the ground of lack of substantive jurisdiction in relation to him, but he does not have the duty to exhaust arbitral procedures (contrast section 70, above).

- By *section 73* (Loss of right to object), a party may lose his right to object under section 67 if he continues to take part in the proceedings without making his objection immediately or within the allowed time unless he shows that when he took part in the proceedings he did not know and could not with reasonable diligence have discovered the grounds for the objection. Section 73 also provides that where the tribunal rules that it has substantive jurisdiction and a party to the proceedings who could have questioned that ruling by any available arbitral process or by challenging the award does not do so within the time allowed, he may not object later to the tribunal's substantive jurisdiction on any ground which was the subject of that ruling.

Secondly, there is the serious irregularity challenge under section 68. The term "serious irregularity" has taken the place of "misconduct" used in earlier legislation.

The leading provision is that a party to arbitral proceedings may (upon notice to the other parties and to the tribunal) apply to the court challenging an award on the ground of serious irregularity affecting the tribunal, the proceedings or the award.

Serious irregularity means an irregularity of one or more of the following kinds *which the court considers has caused or will cause substantial injustice to the applicant*:

- failure by the tribunal to comply with section 33 (General duty of tribunal);
- the tribunal exceeding its own powers (but not by exceeding its substantive jurisdiction, which is dealt with by section 67);
- failure by the tribunal to conduct the proceedings in accordance with the procedure agreed by the parties (*e.g.* if the parties agreed that there should be a hearing and the tribunal made its award without a hearing);
- failure by the tribunal to deal with all the issues which were put to it;
- any arbitral or other institution (*e.g.* the ICC or LCIA) or person vested by the parties with powers in relation to the proceedings or the award (*e.g.* the President of the Law Society) exceeding its powers;
- uncertainty or ambiguity as to the effect of the award;
- the award being obtained by fraud or the award or the way in which it was procured being contrary to public policy;
- failure to comply with the requirements as to the form of the award; or
- any irregularity in the conduct of the proceedings or in the

award which is admitted by the tribunal or by any arbitral or other institution or person vested by the parties with powers in relation to the proceedings or the award.

If there is shown to be serious irregularity affecting the tribunal, the proceedings or the award, the court may (i) remit the award to the tribunal, in whole or in part, for reconsideration, or (ii) set the award aside, in whole or in part, or (iii) declare the award to be of no effect, in whole or in part, but the court must not exercise its power under (ii) or (iii) unless it is satisfied that it would be inappropriate to remit under (i).

The leave of the court is required for any appeal from a decision of the court under section 68.

As with section 67, there must be added to these provisions of section 68 the supplementary and other provisions in sections 70 to 73 insofar as they relate to applications under section 68.

The provisions of *section 70* applicable to section 68 are precisely the same as those applicable to section 67 (see above, points (1) to (5) under section 70)

The provisions of *section 71* relate to the effect of a court order for remission to the tribunal, and for declaring the award to be of no effect—powers which did not arise under section 67.

Section 71 provides that where the award is *remitted* to the tribunal, in whole or in part, for reconsideration, the tribunal must make a fresh award in respect of the matters remitted within three months of the date of the order for remission or such longer or shorter period as the court may direct.

Where the award is *declared to be of no effect*, in whole or in part, the court may also order that any provision that an award is a condition precedent to the bringing of legal proceedings in respect of a matter to which the arbitration agreement applies, is of no effect as regards the subject-matter of the award or the relevant part of it.

The provisions of *section 72* save the right of a person, alleged to be a party to arbitral proceedings but who takes no part in the proceedings, to challenge the award by an application under section 68 on the ground of serious irregularity. In other respects section 72 applies to section 68 in the same way as to section 67.

Section 73 (Loss of right to object) provides, in relation to section 68, that if a party to arbitral proceedings continues to take part in the arbitral proceedings without making immediately or within the allowed time any objection:

- that the proceedings have been improperly conducted,
- that there has been a failure to comply with the arbitration agreement or with any provision of this Part of the Act, or

- that there has been any other irregularity affecting the tribunal or the proceedings,

then he may not raise that objection later before the tribunal or the court, unless he shows that, at the time when he continued to take part in the proceedings, he did not know and could not with reasonable diligence have discovered the grounds for the objection.

(C) Appeal on a Point of Law

Section 69, which is not mandatory and replaces section 1 of the Arbitration Act 1979, provides that unless otherwise agreed by the parties, a party to arbitral proceedings may (upon notice to the other parties and to the tribunal) appeal to the court on a question of law arising out of an award.

An agreement to dispense with reasons for the tribunal's award is considered an agreement to exclude the court's jurisdiction.

Under the Act of 1979, three special categories of cases (maritime disputes and disputes arising out of insurance contracts or commodity contracts) could not be excluded from the court's jurisdiction, but under the Act of 1996 these exclusions no longer apply.

An appeal cannot be brought under section 69 except with either the agreement of all the other parties to the proceedings or the leave of the court.

Section 69 codifies "guidelines" which had come to be recognised by House of Lords cases on the Act of 1979—*Pioneer Shipping BTP Tioxide Ltd (The "Nema")* (1982) and *Antaios Cia Naviera S.A. v. Salen Rederierna A.B. (The "Antaios")* (1985). The section provides that leave to appeal can be given only if the court is satisfied that:

(1) the determination of the question will substantially affect the rights of one or more of the parties,

(2) the question is one which the tribunal was asked to determine,

(3) on the basis of findings of fact in the award, (i) the decision of the tribunal on the question is obviously wrong, or (ii) the question is one of general public importance and the decision of the tribunal is at least open to serious doubt, and

(4) despite the agreement of the parties to resolve the matter by arbitration, it is just and proper in all the circumstances for the court to determine the question.

An application for leave to appeal must identify the question of law and state the grounds on which it is alleged that leave to appeal should be granted.

The court must determine an application for leave to appeal without a hearing, unless it appears to the court that a hearing is required.

The leave of the court is required for any appeal from a decision of the court to grant or refuse leave to appeal.

On an appeal under section 69 the court may by order (i) confirm the award, (ii) vary the award, (iii) remit the award to the tribunal, in whole or in part, for reconsideration in the light of the court's determination, or (iv) set aside the award in whole or in part. However, the court must not exercise its power under (iv) unless it is satisfied that it would be inappropriate to remit the matters in question to the tribunal for reconsideration under (iii).

The decision of the court hearing an appeal under section 69 is to be treated as a judgment of the court for the purposes of a further appeal, but leave of the court is required for such a further appeal, and that leave is not to be given unless the court considers that the question is one of general importance or is one which for some other special reason should be considered by the Court of Appeal. The *Nema* and *Antaios* guidelines do not apply to applications for leave to appeal to the Court of Appeal (*Geogas S.A. v. Tramma Gas Ltd (The "Baleares")* (1991, C.A.)).

The supplementary provisions in *section 70* apply to an appeal under section 69 as they apply to an application under section 67 (see points 1. to 5. under section 70, above).

Similarly, *section 71*, relating to the effect of the order of the court provides that:

- Where the award is varied, the variation has effect as part of the tribunal's award.
- Where the award is remitted to the tribunal, in whole or in part, for reconsideration, the tribunal must make a fresh award in respect of the matters remitted within three months of the date of the order for remission or such longer or shorter period as the court may direct.
- Where the award is set aside, in whole or in part, the court may also order that any provision that an award is a condition precedent to the bringing of legal proceedings in respect of a matter to which the arbitration agreement applies, is of no effect as regards the subject-matter of the award or the relevant part of the award.

FURTHER READING

Russell on Arbitration, chap. 8 ("The Role of the Court after the Award").
Merkin, Chaps. 17 ("Enforcement of Arbitration Awards"), 18 ("Challenging the Proceedings and the Award") and 19 ("Judicial Review of Errors of Law in Arbitral Awards").

CHAPTER 8

OTHER PROVISIONS RELATING TO ARBITRATION

INTRODUCTION

WHILE the principal Part of the Act, Part I, is headed "Arbitration pursuant to an arbitration agreement" and its provisions have been considered so far, Part II is headed "Other provisions relating to arbitration" and is the subject-matter of this chapter. Part II consists of sections 85 to 98 of the Act.

The topics are:

(a) Domestic arbitration agreements (sections 85 to 88);

(b) Consumer arbitration agreements (sections 89 to 91);

(c) Small claims arbitration in the county court (section 92);

(d) Appointment of judges as arbitrators (section 93); and

(e) Statutory arbitrations (sections 94 to 98).

(A) DOMESTIC ARBITRATION AGREEMENTS

Sections 85 to 87 have not been brought into force. They are excepted from the Arbitration Act 1996 (Commencement No. 1) Order 1996 (S.I. 1996 No. 3145 (C. 96)), which brought the rest of the Act into force on January 31, 1997.

The leading provision in this group of sections is that in the case of a domestic arbitration agreement the provisions of Part I would have been modified in accordance with sections 86 and 87 (section 85).

"Domestic arbitration agreement" for this purpose means an arbitration agreement to which none of the parties is:

- either an individual who is a national of, or habitually resident in, a state other than the United Kingdom, or
- a body corporate which is incorporated in, or whose central control and management is exercised in, a state other than the United Kingdom,

and under which the seat of the arbitration (if it has been designated or determined) is in the United Kingdom.

The first modification which would have been made if these provisions had been brought into force relates to the stay of legal proceedings. Section 9, which is in Part I, provides that the court *must* grant a stay unless satisfied that the arbitration agreement is null and void, inoperative, or incapable of being performed. Section 86 adds an alternative to that provision—which in effect gives the court a discretion; it provides that the court *must* grant a stay unless satisfied:

(i) that the arbitration agreement is null and void, inoperative, or incapable of being performed, *or*

(ii) that there are other sufficient grounds for not requiring the parties to abide by the arbitration agreement.

The court *may* treat as a sufficient ground under (ii), above, the fact that the applicant is or was at any material time not ready and willing to do all things necessary for the proper conduct of the arbitration or of any other dispute resolution procedures required to be exhausted before resorting to arbitration.

For the purposes of section 86 the question whether an arbitration agreement is a domestic arbitration agreement is determined by reference to the facts at the time when the legal proceedings are commenced.

The second modification which would have applied is in section 87 and relates to the effectiveness of a domestic arbitration agreement to exclude the court's jurisdiction under section 45 (Determination of preliminary point of law) or section 69 (Appeal on a point of law). Sections 45 and 69 are non-mandatory and so apply "unless otherwise agreed by the parties". Section 87 provides that any agreement to exclude the jurisdiction of the court under section 45 or section 69 would not have been effective unless entered into after the commencement of the arbitral proceedings.

For the purposes of section 87 the question whether an arbitration agreement is a domestic arbitration agreement is determined by reference to the facts at the time when the agreement is entered into.

Section 88 provides that the Secretary of State may by statutory instrument repeal or amend the provisions of sections 85 to 87.

(B) CONSUMER ARBITRATION AGREEMENTS

Sections 89 to 91 replace the Consumer Arbitration Agreements Act 1988. They apply to Scotland as well as to England and Wales and Northern Ireland (section 108).

The purpose of the Act of 1988 was to make unenforceable an arbitration agreement to which a consumer was a party and which fell within county court limits, if the arbitration agreement had been entered into before the dispute arose.

A parallel regime came into existence on July 1, 1995 when the United Kingdom implemented an E.C. directive (Directive 93/13) by enacting the Unfair Terms in Consumer Contracts Regulations 1994 (S.I. 1994 No. 3159). These Regulations were repealed and replaced by the Unfair Terms in Consumer Contracts Regulations 1999 (S.I. 1999 No. 2083), which were brought into force on October 1, 1999.

The effect of the Act of 1996 is to base the protection of consumers wholly on the Regulations by extending the application of the Regulations to a term which constitutes an arbitration agreement (section 89) and repealing the whole of the Act of 1988 (section 107 and Schedule 4).

Section 89 defines "arbitration agreement" for the purposes of these provisions as an agreement to submit to arbitration *present or future disputes or differences (whether or not contractual)* and the provisions apply *whatever the law applicable to the arbitration agreement.* The points in italics are an extension to the provisions in the Act of 1988: that earlier legislation concerned only an arbitration agreement which had been entered into before the dispute arose, and whereas the Act of 1988 applied only to domestic arbitrations, the Regulations apply to all contracts which come before the United Kingdom court, whatever the law applicable to them.

The Regulations apply whether the *consumer* is a legal person or a natural person (section 90). This provision is an extension of the Regulations themselves, which define "consumer" as meaning a *natural person* who, in making a contract to which the Regulations apply, is acting for purposes which are outside his trade, business or profession (Regulation 3).

The Regulations apply to *unfair terms* in contracts concluded between a *seller or a supplier* and a consumer (Regulation 4). "Seller or supplier" is defined in the Regulations as meaning any natural or legal person who, in contracts covered by the Regulations, is acting for purposes relating to his trade, business or profession, whether publicly owned or privately owned (Regulation 3).

The effect of an unfair term in a contract concluded with a consumer by a seller or supplier is that the term is not binding on the consumer, though the contract continues to bind the parties if it is capable of continuing in existence without the unfair term (Regulation 8).

A contractual term which has not been *individually negotiated* is regarded as unfair if, contrary to the requirement of *good faith*, it causes a *significant imbalance* in the parties' rights and obligations arising under the contract, to the detriment of the consumer. A term must always be regarded as not having been individually negotiated where it has been drafted in advance and the consumer has therefore not been able to influence the substance of the term. It is for the seller or supplier who claims that a term was individually negotiated to show that it was. Schedule 2 to the Regulations contains an indicative and non-exhaustive list of terms which may be regarded as unfair (Regulation 5). The last in that list ((q)) is a term excluding or hindering the consumer's right to take legal action or exercise any other legal remedy, particularly by requiring the consumer to take disputes exclusively to arbitration not covered by legal provisions. For the full text of the Regulations see Appendix 3, below.

The Act in section 91 provides that a term in an arbitration agreement is unfair for the purposes of the Regulations if it relates to a claim for a pecuniary remedy which does not exceed an amount specified by statutory instrument. The amount was fixed at £3,000 by the Unfair Arbitration Agreements (Specified Amount) Order 1996 (S.I. 1996 No. 3211) and was increased to £5,000 by the Unfair Arbitration Agreements (Specified Amount) Order 1999 (S.I. 1999 No. 2167), with effect from January 1, 2000.

(C) Small Claims Arbitration in the County Court

Section 92 makes it clear that Part I of the Act of 1996 does not apply to arbitration under section 64 of the County Courts Act 1984. The procedure and rules of evidence of arbitration conducted under the Act of 1984 are in the County Court Rules.

Small claims of £1,000 or less are automatically referred to arbitration unless the court otherwise orders because of specific circumstances. The district judge himself will be the arbitrator unless the court order making the reference provides otherwise. An outside arbitrator will not be employed without the consent of both parties.

Claims over £1,000 may be referred to arbitration on the application of one of the parties.

The hearing of the arbitration is informal and the strict rules of evidence do not apply. The tribunal may adopt any procedure which is considered fair and which gives each party an equal opportunity to have his case presented.

The award is entered as a judgment in the proceedings and is as binding and effective as if it had been given by the judge.

(D) Appointment of Judges as Arbitrators

Section 93 permits a judge of the Commercial Court or an official referee, if in all the circumstances he sees fit, to accept appointment as a sole arbitrator or as umpire. The term used is "judge-arbitrator" (Schedule 2). He cannot act as a member of an arbitral tribunal, but only as a sole arbitrator or umpire. The parties do not have the right to make an appointment.

A judge of the Commercial Court must not accept appointment unless the Lord Chief Justice has informed him that, having regard to the state of business in the High Court and the Crown Court, he can be made available. There is a similar restriction on an official referee: he must not accept appointment unless the Lord Chief Justice has informed him that, having regard to the state of official referees' business, he can be made available. Appointments are rare because the heavy workload hinders the availability.

The fees payable for the services of a judge-arbitrator are taken in the High Court.

The provisions of Part I of the Act apply to judge-arbitrators with the modifications specified in Schedule 2 to the Act: in particular, all references in Part I of the Act to the court are to be construed as references to the Court of Appeal, and where there is an appeal from the court to the Court of Appeal (determination of a preliminary point of jurisdiction under section 32, determination of a preliminary point of law under section 45 and appeal on a point of law under section 69), the appeal goes to the House of Lords.

(E) Statutory Arbitrations

Sections 94 to 98 consist of provisions relating to the extent to which the provisions of Part I of the Act apply to statutory arbitrations, *i.e.* to arbitrations under an "enactment" (an Act of Parliament or subordinate legislation) passed before or after the commencement of the Act of 1996.

The leading provision is that Part I does not apply to a statutory arbitration if, and to the extent that, the application:

- is inconsistent with the provisions of the enactment concerned, with any rules or procedure authorised or recognised by it, or
- is excluded by any other enactment (section 94).

Section 95 provides that Part I applies to a statutory arbitration:

- as if the arbitration was under an arbitration agreement and as if the enactment was that agreement, and
- as if the persons by and against whom a claim is made under the enactment were parties to the agreement.

Section 95 also provides that every statutory arbitration must be taken to have its seat in England and Wales or Northern Ireland. This is to be linked with the provision in section 2: "The provisions of this Part apply where the seat of the arbitration is in England and Wales or Northern Ireland". The seat of a statutory arbitration does not therefore require to be designated under section 3.

Section 96 specifies provisions of Part I which apply to a statutory arbitration only with adaptations, and section 97 specifies provisions of Part I which do not apply at all to a statutory arbitration.

Section 98 enables regulations to make further adaptations and exclusions of the provisions of Part I, both in relation to existing and future statutory arbitrations. The regulations would be made by statutory instrument and would be subject to annulment by a resolution of either House of Parliament.

Further Reading

Russell on Arbitration, Chaps. 2 ("The Arbitration Agreement") and 4 ("The Tribunal") and Appendix 4 ("Statutory Arbitration").

Merkin, Chaps. 1 ("The Framework of Arbitration Law") and 8 "The Office of Arbitrator").

CHAPTER 9

RECOGNITION AND ENFORCEMENT OF CERTAIN FOREIGN AWARDS

INTRODUCTION

PART III of the Act, consisting of sections 99 to 104, relates to the enforcement of Geneva Convention awards (section 99) and to the recognition and enforcement of New York Convention awards (sections 100 to 104). The provisions on Geneva Convention awards effect a continuation of Part II of the Arbitration Act 1950 (which Part is not repealed by the Act of 1996), while the provisions on New York Convention awards are derived from the Arbitration Act 1975, which is wholly repealed, except for Scotland.

A brief account is added at the end of this chapter of institutions which have an important role in international arbitrations.

GENEVA CONVENTION AWARDS

Section 99 provides that Part II of the Arbitration Act 1950 (Enforcement of certain foreign awards) continues to apply in relation to *foreign awards within the meaning of that Part, which are not also New York Convention awards.* Part II also continues to apply to Scotland.

The provisions of Part II, along with the First and Second Schedules, are reproduced in Appendix 3 to *Russell on Arbitration* but they are now applicable to only a few States, because of the stipulation in section 99, based on Article VII of the New York Convention, that the Geneva Protocol and the Geneva Convention cease to have effect between States bound by the New York Convention.

Section 35 of the Act of 1950 provides that a foreign award is one made:

- in pursuance of an arbitration agreement to which the Geneva Protocol (set out in the First Schedule to the Act) applies; and
- between persons who are subject to the jurisdiction of different Powers with which the United Kingdom has made reciprocal provisions and which have been declared by Order in Council to be parties to the Geneva Convention (set out in the Second Schedule to the Act); and
- in a territory in respect of which the United Kingdom has made reciprocal provisions and which has been declared by Order in Council to be a territory to which the Geneva Convention applies.

The Geneva Protocol which comprises the First Schedule is the "Protocol on Arbitration Clauses", which was signed on behalf of the United Kingdom at a meeting of the Assembly of the League of Nations in 1923. The Geneva Convention which comprises the Second Schedule is the "Convention on the Execution of Foreign Arbitral Awards", which was signed on behalf of the United Kingdom at Geneva in 1927.

The Geneva instruments became operative only where reciprocal provisions were made between the two States concerned. Orders in Council, in the form of Arbitration (Foreign Awards) Orders, were made from time to time, specifying the Powers which were parties to the Geneva Convention and the territories to which the Geneva Convention applied and revoking earlier Orders, *e.g.* the Arbitration (Foreign Awards) Order 1978 (S.I. 1978 No. 186).

The Protocol declares that the States which are parties to it ("the Contracting States") recognise the validity of arbitration agreements made between parties who are subject to the jurisdiction of different Contracting States, whether or not the arbitration takes place in a country to whose jurisdiction none of the parties is subject. The arbitral procedure is governed by the will of the parties and by the law of the country in whose territory the arbitration takes place. Each Contracting State undertakes to ensure the execution by its authorities and in accordance with its national laws of arbitral awards made in its own territory. Where there is a valid arbitration agreement capable of being carried into effect, the courts of the

Contracting Parties *must*, on the application of a party to the arbitration agreement, refer the dispute to the arbitrators unless the agreement or the arbitration cannot proceed or becomes inoperative.

The Convention provides that in the territories of the parties to the Convention ("the High Contracting Parties"), an arbitral award made under an agreement covered by the Protocol is recognised as binding and must be enforced in accordance with the rules of procedure of the territory where the award is relied upon, provided the award has been made in a territory of one of the High Contracting Parties and between persons who are subject to the jurisdiction of one of the High Contracting Parties. To obtain recognition or enforcement certain conditions must be fulfilled, the one which has caused most difficulty being the condition that the recognition or enforcement must not be contrary to the public policy or *to the principles of the law* of the country in which it is sought to be relied upon.

New York Convention Awards

Sections 100 to 104 re-enact with some amendment the provisions of the Arbitration Act 1975, which gave effect in the United Kingdom to the New York Convention on the Recognition and Enforcement of Foreign Arbitral Awards adopted by the United Nations Conference on International Commercial Arbitration in 1958. The Act of 1975, which still applies to Scotland, is reproduced in Appendix 3 to *Russell on Arbitration.*

Section 100 provides that in Part III of the Act "New York Convention award" means an award made, in pursuance of an arbitration agreement, in the territory of a state (other than the United Kingdom) which is a party to the New York Convention.

In that definition "arbitration agreement" means an arbitration agreement in writing, and an award is treated as "made" at the seat of the arbitration, regardless of where it was signed, despatched or delivered to any of the parties. The effect is to reverse the decision of the House of Lords in *Hiscox v. Outhwaite* (1992), in which an award was held to have been made in France merely because it was signed there, though the arbitration had been conducted in London and had no connection with France. "Agreement in writing" and "seat of the arbitration" have the same meaning as in Part I of the Act. Orders in Council are conclusive evidence as to the states or territories specified in them.

Section 100 is derived from section 7 of the Act of 1975, under which the following Orders in Council were made—the Arbitration (Foreign Awards) Order 1979 (1979 S.I. No. 304), the Arbitration (Foreign Awards) Order 1984 (1984 S.I. No. 1168), the Arbitration (Foreign Awards) Order 1989 (1989 S.I. No. 1348), and the Arbitration (Foreign Awards) Order 1993 (1993 S.I. No. 1256).

By section 101 a New York Convention award is recognised as binding on the persons as between whom it is made and may therefore be relied on by those persons by way of defence, set-off or otherwise in any legal proceedings in England and Wales or Northern Ireland. The award may, by leave of the court be enforced in the same way as a judgment or order of the court, and where leave is given, judgment may be entered in terms of the award. This section is derived from section 3 of the Act of 1975. "Legal proceedings" is defined in section 82 as "civil proceedings in the High Court or a county court", but that definition applies only to terms in Part I of the Act, and so "legal proceedings" in section 101 may extend to other legal proceedings, such as an arbitration.

On the evidence which must be produced by a party seeking the recognition or enforcement of a New York Convention award, section 102, reproducing section 4 of the Act of 1975, provides that the party must produce the duly authenticated original award or a duly certified copy of it and the original arbitration agreement or a duly certified copy of it, and if the award or agreement is in a foreign language, the party must also produce a translation of it certified by an official or sworn translator or by a diplomatic or consular agent.

Section 103, derived from section 5 of the Act of 1975 and Article V of the Convention, sets out the limited number of cases in which recognition or enforcement of a New York Convention award may be refused. It provides that recognition or enforcement may be refused if the person against whom it is invoked proves that:

- a party to the arbitration agreement was (under the law applicable to him) under some incapacity;
- the arbitration agreement was not valid under the law to which the parties subjected it or, failing any indication, under the law of the country where the award was made;
- he was not given proper notice of the appointment of the arbitrator or of the arbitration proceedings or was otherwise unable to present his case;
- the award deals with a difference not contemplated by or not falling within the terms of the submission or contains decisions on matters beyond the scope of the submission (but the award may be recognised or enforced to the extent that it contains decisions on matters submitted which can be separated from those on matters not submitted);

- the composition of the arbitral tribunal or the arbitral procedure was not in accordance with the agreement of the parties or, failing such agreement, with the law of the country in which the arbitration took place;
- the award has not yet become binding on the parties or has been set aside or suspended by a competent authority of the country in which, or under the law of which, it was made, (but where an application for setting aside or suspension has been made, the court before which the award is sought to be relied upon may, if it considers it proper, adjourn the decision on the recognition or enforcement, and may also, on the application of the party claiming recognition or enforcement, order the other party to give suitable security);
- the award is in respect of a matter which is not capable of settlement by arbitration, or if it would be contrary to public policy to recognise or enforce the award.

Recognition or enforcement is mandatory unless one of the specified grounds is proved, and the onus of proof is on the person against whom the award is invoked.

Section 104 provides that nothing in the preceding provisions of Part III affects any right to rely on or to enforce a New Convention award at common law or under section 66. There is a similar provision in section 6 of the Act of 1975.

Section 104 leaves open the possibility at common law of bringing an action founded on the arbitration award. If there is no arguable defence, the court may enter summary judgment on the basis of documents and sworn depositions.

Section 66 (which is in Part I of the Act) provides that an award may *by leave of the court* be enforced in the same manner as a judgment or order of the court. The court has therefore a discretion. The distinction between that section and the provisions in Part III is that recognition and enforcement under Part III can only be refused in the cases set out in section 103, above. The result may be that section 66 provides greater opportunity for refusal.

International Chamber of Commerce

The International Chamber of Commerce ("ICC"), established in 1923, has its administrative centre in Paris. It has a commanding position amongst the numerous bodies which provide arbitration services to businessmen engaged in international trade. It has its own Court of Arbitration, appointed by its council. The Court operates the Rules of Arbitration of the ICC (1998). (See *Russell on Arbitration*, Appendix 4.)

The ICC Rules provide for optional conciliation in the first instance when a dispute arises. If an amicable solution cannot be reached, the dispute is referred to an arbitration panel, which is subject to the general supervisory role of the Court of Arbitration.

The Court's functions under the Rules include the following:

- appointing the arbitration panel if the parties do not do so, and confirming the appointment of every arbitrator;
- adjudicating on the validity of the agreement to arbitrate;
- fixing the costs of the arbitration;
- determining the place of the arbitration if the parties themselves do not do so; and
- scrutinising and approving the draft of the arbitrators' award.

LONDON COURT OF INTERNATIONAL ARBITRATION

The London Court of International Arbitration ("LCIA"), formerly named the London Court of Arbitration, revised its rules in 1998. The arbitration is conducted by a panel of arbitrators in terms of the LCIA Rules.

The Court's general supervisory powers are mainly less extensive than those exercised by the Court under the ICC Rules. The main functions of the Court are:

- appointing or confirming the appointment of the arbitral panel; and
- confirming the tribunal's directions as to costs.

The award and the correction of any errors in it are matters for the panel itself.

ARBITRATION (INTERNATIONAL INVESTMENT DISPUTES) ACT 1966

The Arbitration (International Investment Disputes) Act 1966 gave effect in the United Kingdom to the Convention on the Settlement of Investment Disputes between States and Nationals of Other States ("the Washington Convention") 1965.

The Convention provided for the formation of an International Centre for Settlement of Investment Disputes ("ICSID"). The Centre makes available to Contracting States and foreign investors who are nationals of other Contracting States facilities for the settlement, on a voluntary basis, of investment disputes in accordance with rules laid down in the Convention.

The Convention is set out in a Schedule to the Act.

MULTILATERAL INVESTMENT GUARANTEE AGENCY ACT 1988

This Act gave force in English law to the Convention establishing the Multilateral Investment Guarantee Agency 1985. Disputes are governed by ICSID principles.

THE INTERNATIONAL BAR ASSOCIATION

The International Bar Association ("IBA") has produced Supplementary Rules of Evidence intended to be incorporated into standard arbitration rules governing international commercial arbitrations to supplement those rules and fill in gaps in the arbitration laws of many countries where domestic rules are not comprehensive. The Rules, for instance, deal with basic issues such as the production of documents, witnesses and the powers of arbitrators.

UNCITRAL ARBITRATION RULES

The United Nations Commission on International Trade Law ("UNCITRAL") was established by the United Nations in 1966 for the purpose of harmonising international trade law. Its work has extended to the making of rules for the formation of contracts and for the international sale of goods. In 1976 it published Arbitration Rules, and these were supplemented by conciliation rules in 1980 and by the publication of guidelines on their operation in 1982.

UNCITRAL's outstanding contribution to the law of arbitration is the Model Law on International Commercial Arbitration ("Model Law") which it adopted in 1985. It was the result of a comprehensive study into the various arbitration laws throughout the world and was intended to provide a model which would lead to greater uniformity.

English law has not adopted the Model Law, but much of the Act of 1996 reflects its format and provisions. Scotland, on the other hand, adopted the Model Law by the Law Reform (Miscellaneous Provisions) (Scotland) Act 1990.

For the full text of the Model Law with Commentary see *Russell on Arbitration*, Appendix 5 ("Comparison between the Arbitration Act 1996 and the UNCITRAL Model Law on International Commercial Arbitration ('Model Law')").

Further Reading

Russell on Arbitration, Chaps. 1 ("Introduction"), 2 ("The Arbitration Agreement"), 6 ("The Award") and 8 ("The Role of the Court after the Award") and Appendices 3 (for Arbitration Act 1950 Part II and First and Second Schedules) and 5 ("Comparison between the Arbitration Act 1996 and the UNCITRAL Model Law on International Commercial Arbitration ('Model Law')").

Merkin, Chaps 1 ("The Framework of Arbitration Law") and 17 ("Enforcement of Arbitration Awards").

Lord and Salzedo, Appendices 1 (for Arbitration Act 1950 Part II and First and Second Schedules), 5 ("United Nations Conference on International Commercial Arbitration: Convention on the Recognition and Enforcement of Foreign Arbitral Awards, New York 1958") and 6 ("UNCITRAL Model Law on International Commercial Arbitration (As adopted by the United Nations Commission on International Trade Law on June 21, 1985)").

Harris, Planterose and Tecks, Appendix for the Arbitration Act 1950 Part II and First and Second Schedules.

CHAPTER 10

AN OUTLINE OF THE SCOTS LAW OF ARBITRATION

INTRODUCTION

THE purpose of this chapter is not to give an account of the Scots law of arbitration but merely to indicate those major respects in which it differs from English law.

Scotland does not yet have any single Act corresponding to the Arbitration Act 1996, but there has been some move towards comprehensive reform of the Scots law of arbitration over recent years. A draft Bill is in existence (see Appendix V to Fraser Davidson, *Arbitration*) but so far has not been introduced into the Scottish Parliament. By the Scotland Act 1998 arbitration is now a devolved matter.

In 1986, the Lord Advocate, after consultation with the Secretary of State for Trade and Industry, established the Scottish Advisory Committee on Arbitration Law, with the following terms of reference:

- to advise on whether, and if so to what extent, the provisions of the draft Model Law adopted by a Working Group of the United Nations Commission on International Trade Law in

February 1984 should be implemented in Scotland and what measures should be taken for that purpose;

- to examine the operation of the system of arbitration in Scotland in the light of the Model Law and to make recommendations regarding any legislative or other steps which the Committee considers should be taken to improve the system of arbitration in Scotland; and
- to consider the implications for Scotland of any recommendations or advice which might be given by the Mustill Committee, and to advise. (The Mustill Committee was the Department of Trade and Industry's Departmental Advisory Committee established to reform English arbitration law under the successive chairmanship of Lord Mustill, Lord Steyn and Lord Justice Saville. The Arbitration Act of 1996 resulted from that Committee.)

In 1989 the Scottish Advisory Committee submitted a report to the Lord Advocate, recommending that the UNCITRAL Model Law should be enacted in Scotland, and this recommendation was followed by section 66 of, and Schedule 7 to, the Law Reform (Miscellaneous Provisions) (Scotland) Act 1990 (see Davidson, above).

The Committee then turned its attention to its other terms of reference and in 1996 submitted a further report to the Lord Advocate on legislation for domestic arbitration in Scotland. Appended to the report is a draft Arbitration (Scotland) Bill of 34 sections and two Schedules. The purpose was not to produce a "code" but to consolidate earlier provisions and add new provisions which put beyond doubt the law in some areas where there was uncertainty, thus creating a strong legislative framework for arbitration in Scotland while retaining as much flexibility as possible for matters which were not part of that framework.

Terminology

The terms "arbiter" and "oversman" correspond in Scots law to the English terms "arbitrator" and "umpire", respectively. In Scots law an alternative term for "award" is "decree-arbitral".

Sources

The general Scots law of arbitration is almost wholly common law. The arbitration code now comprising Part I of the Arbitration Act 1996 does not apply to Scotland. Sections 89, 90 and 91 (Consumer arbitration agreements) in Part II apply to Scotland, and the repeal of the Arbitration Act 1975 does not extend to Scotland (section 108). Part II of the Arbitration Act 1950 continues to apply to Scotland as it does to England (section 99).

Such statutory provisions as do affect the Scots law of arbitration deal with specific aspects only and are to be found in an odd assortment of legislation—the Articles of Regulation of 1695 which were authorised by an Act of the Parliament of Scotland, the Arbitration (Scotland) Act 1894 (see Appendix 4 to this book), section 3 of the Administration of Justice (Scotland) Act 1972 (see Appendix 5 to this book), section 17 of the Law Reform (Miscellaneous Provisions) (Scotland) Act 1980 and Schedule 7 to the Law Reform (Miscellaneous Provisions) (Scotland) Act 1990.

The Courts and Arbitration

There was a marked distinction between English and Scots law in the attitude of the courts to arbitration. The Act of 1996, however, has done much to change that distinction, one of the general principles of English law being now the mandatory provision that in matters governed by Part I of the Act the court is not to intervene except as provided by Part I (section 1).

Enforcement of arbitration agreement

Before the Act of 1996, one of the leading provisions of English arbitration law was that if a party to an arbitration agreement commenced court proceedings, the court *might* make an order staying these proceedings (Arbitration Act 1950, section 4). In Scotland the court had no such discretion: it was bound to give effect to the parties' agreement to arbitrate by "sisting" the court proceedings.

Of the differing approaches in the two legal systems Lord Dunedin said in the House of Lords case *Sanderson & Son v. Armour & Co. Ltd* (1922):

> "The English common law doctrine,—eventually swept away by the Arbitration Act of 1889—that a contract to oust the jurisdiction of the Courts was against public policy and invalid, never obtained in Scotland. In the same way, the right which in England pertains to the Court under that Act to apply or not to apply the arbitration clause in its discretion never was the right of the Court in Scotland. If the parties have contracted to arbitrate, to arbitration they must go."

The mandatory provision in section 9 of the Act of 1996 brings the English law on this point into line with the Scots common law.

Section 9 provides that a party to an arbitration agreement against whom court proceedings are brought may apply to the court to stay the proceedings, and the court *must* grant a stay (unless satisfied that the arbitration agreement is null and void, inoperative, or incapable of being performed).

Questions of law

The tradition of English law was that an arbitrator's power to decide questions of law was controlled by the court and a purported exclusion by agreement of the court's control was void and unenforceable. The situation was described in a famous observation by Scrutton L.J. in *Czarnikow v. Roth Schmidt & Co.* (1922):

> [The Courts] "do not allow the agreement of private parties to oust the jurisdiction of the King's Courts. Arbitrators, unless expressly otherwise authorised, have to apply the laws of England. . . . There must be no Alsatia in England where the King's writ does not run."

In Scots law, on the other hand, the arbiter was at common law final both on questions of fact and on questions of law and there was no right of appeal to the courts. A well-known passage is that in Lord Jeffrey's opinion in *Mitchell v. Cable* (1848):

> "On every matter touching the merits of the case, the judgment of the arbiter is beyond our control; and beyond question or cavil. He may believe what nobody else believes, and he may disbelieve what all the world believes. He may overlook or flagrantly misapply the most ordinary principles of law; and there is no appeal for those who have chosen to subject themselves to his despotic power."

(These are, however, extreme words when taken out of context; it should be borne in mind that Lord Jeffrey went on to explain that a decree-arbitral can stand only when the arbiter has done his duty "fairly", *i.e.* has dealt equally with both parties. In *Mitchell v. Cable* the arbiter was held not to have satisfied this test because he had considered proof from one party without allowing the other party a fair opportunity of bringing forward his counter-proof.)

Scots law had originally no special or stated case procedure corresponding to the much criticised English special case procedure, which was abolished by the Act of 1979.

The absence of "special case" procedure from Scots law was highlighted by *James Miller and Partners Ltd v. Whitworth Street Estates (Manchester) Ltd* (1970), in which the House of Lords held that the law governing the arbitration proceedings, as distinct from the proper law of the contract, was Scots law and that the arbiter had therefore been entitled to refuse a request from one of the parties to state his award in the form of a special case.

Two years later, however, the special or stated case procedure was introduced to Scotland by section 3 of the Administration of Justice (Scotland) Act 1972 (see Appendix 5 to this book). Unlike the former English provision in section 21 of the Act of 1950, the Scottish provision was made "subject to express provision to the contrary in an agreement to refer to arbitration", *i.e.*, it could be contracted out of.

The provision is that the arbiter or oversman *may*, on the application of a party to the arbitration, at any stage in the arbitration state a case for the opinion of the Court of Session on any question of law arising in the arbitration, and the arbiter or oversman *must* do so if the party applies to the Court of Session and that court directs a case to be stated.

The application must be made at a *stage in the arbitration* (*e.g.* after the arbiter has issued proposed findings); it is no longer competent after the arbiter has issued his final award (*Fairlie Yacht Slip Co. Ltd v. Lumsden* (1977)).

Before April 1973 (when the provision was brought into force) stated cases in Scots law had been confined to statutory arbitrations; for example, in *Mitchell-Gill v. Buchan* (1921) the court held, in relation to a stated case under the Agricultural Holdings (Scotland) Act 1908, that an arbiter was not entitled to disregard the answer given by the court on the question of law.

The corresponding provision in English law is now in section 45 of the Act of 1996: unless otherwise agreed by the parties, the court may on the application of a party to arbitral proceedings determine any question of law arising in the course of the proceedings which the court is satisfied substantially affects the rights of one or more of the parties. This provision also may be contracted out of: an agreement to dispense with reasons for the tribunal's award is to be considered as an agreement to exclude the court's jurisdiction under the section. Other conditions must also be fulfilled for successful applications under section 45 (see page 52, above).

Appointment of Arbiters and Oversmen

Statutory provisions relating to the appointment of arbiters and oversmen are:

- the Arbitration (Scotland) Act 1894 (see Appendix 4 to this book), and

- section 17 of the Law Reform (Miscellaneous Provisions) (Scotland) Act 1980.

Arbitration (Scotland) Act 1894

This Act was passed mainly to remedy two deficiencies which had become apparent in the common law.

First, it was a principle of the common law that the appointment of an arbiter involved *delectus personae* (literally "choice of person"), and so the parties had to make a deliberate selection of a named individual and not merely agree that the arbiter would be the holder of a particular office for the time being or would be named by another person. The courts would not, as a general rule, enforce an arbitration agreement in which the arbiter was not named. There were some exceptions to the general rule (*e.g.* the arbitration agreement would be enforceable if the arbitration was necessary for the purpose of giving effect to another contract), but on the whole the common law rule had the unsatisfactory result of bringing before the courts matters which the parties had really intended should be settled by arbitration; *e.g.* an arbitration clause in a contract for the building of the Forth Railway Bridge providing that disputes were to be referred to "the engineer of the Forth Bridge Railway Company for the time being" was held to be unenforceable (*Tancred Arrol & Co. v. The Steel Co. of Scotland Ltd* (1890)).

The second deficiency was that at common law where there was a reference to two arbiters, one appointed by each side, the two arbiters had no implied power to appoint an oversman, and so if the arbiters failed to agree the result was deadlock.

The provisions of the Act are:

- An agreement to refer to arbitration is no longer unenforceable merely because the reference is to a person not named or to a person to be named by another, or to a person described as the holder of an office for the time being (section 1).

- Where there is an agreement to refer to a single arbiter and one of the parties refuses to concur in the nomination and there is no provision in the agreement to resolve the difficulty, then any party to the agreement may apply to the court for an arbiter to be appointed by the court (section 2).

- Where there is an agreement to refer to two arbiters and one of the parties refuses to name an arbiter and there is no provision in the agreement to resolve the difficulty, then the other party may apply to the court for an arbiter to be appointed by the court (section 3).

- Unless the agreement to refer provides otherwise, arbiters have power to name an oversman on whom the reference is to be devolved in the event of their differing in opinion. If the arbiters fail to agree in the nomination of an oversman, any party to the agreement may apply to the court for an oversman to be appointed by the court (section 4).

The Act leaves a number of gaps: the court has no power to appoint an arbiter where the parties have merely agreed to refer "to arbitration" without specifying that the reference is to be to a single arbiter or to two arbiters (*M'Millan & Son Ltd v. Rowan & Co.* (1903)); there is no provision corresponding to section 15 of the Act of 1996 ("If there is no agreement as to the number of arbitrators, the tribunal shall consist of a sole arbitrator"); nor is there any remedy for the situation where the clause of reference names an arbiter and he refuses to act (*British Westinghouse Electric and Manufacturing Co Ltd v. Provost, etc., of Aberdeen* (1906)).

Law Reform (Miscellaneous Provisions) (Scotland) Act 1980, section 17

This section enables a Court of Session judge, if in all the circumstances he thinks fit, to accept appointment as arbiter or as oversman under an arbitration agreement where the dispute appears to him to be of a commercial character. It is a condition of his accepting appointment that the Lord President of the Court of Session has informed him that, having regard to the state of business in that court, he can be made available to do so.

The fees for the judge's services as arbiter or oversman are paid into public funds and are of an amount fixed by statutory instrument, and increased from time to time, the latest being the Appointment of Judges as Arbiters (Fees) (Scotland) Order 1993 (S.I. 1993 No. 3125), operative from January 11, 1994.

The corresponding English provisions are now in section 93 of, and Schedule 2 to, the Act of 1996.

Procedure

Where the procedure is formal, it approximates to the procedure followed in the Scottish courts.

The arbiter fixes a time within which one party must lodge written claims. He then allows a specified time within which the other party must lodge written answers. A "record" (a written document setting out both sides of the dispute) may then be made up, "adjusted" and eventually "closed".

The arbiter then decides what "proof" (*i.e.* evidence) should be allowed. Sometimes it will be necessary for the arbiter to inspect premises or other property in order to inform himself of the matters in dispute, but inadequacy of inspection is not a ground on which an award may be reduced (*i.e.* set aside) by the court (*Johnson v. Lamb* (1981).

The arbiter will almost always allow a hearing to both parties at the conclusion of the proof, and will often issue "proposed findings" so that the parties may have an opportunity to make final "representations" criticising the proposed findings. A further hearing may be allowed for these representations.

There are, as in England, many informal arbitrations in which both a proof and a hearing may be dispensed with and the question decided on the basis of the arbiter's personal inspection only.

The arbiter is bound to adhere to any procedure agreed on by the parties, but he usually has a wide discretion as to the procedure to be followed. The overriding principle is impartiality, which is implied in the nature of his office: he must adopt "equal and even-handed procedure towards both parties alike" (J. M. Bell, *Treatise on the Law of Arbitration in Scotland*, 2nd edition, page 23).

Time Limits and Prorogations

The duration of the submission is a matter for the parties to decide.

Where the submission is a formal deed, it is usual for the arbiter to be given power to decide the dispute "between this and the . . . day of . . . next to come". If the blanks are not filled up, the submission is regarded as lasting (on the authority of Lord Bankton as applied in *Earl of Dunmore v. M'Inturner* (1829)) for a year and a day.

Where there is no reference to any time limit the submission lasts for the 20-year prescriptive period.

Where the submission expressly fixes a time limit without conferring on the arbiter power to extend the time, the submission automatically falls on the expiry of the specified time, unless the parties by express agreement or by their actings extend its duration.

It is usual practice to confer on the arbiter a power of "prorogation", *i.e.* a power to extend the duration of the submission. Such a power requires to be exercised before the fixed time has expired and before the submission has devolved on the oversman. An arbiter has no implied power of prorogation except, possibly, in ancillary submissions (*i.e.* submissions provided for by arbitration clauses in associated contracts) (Irons and Melville, *Treatise on the Law of Arbitration in Scotland*, page 135).

In the absence of agreement to the contrary, a submission terminates on the death of either of the parties.

Enforcement of Award

An award may be enforced by action brought by a party to the arbitration. If the decree-arbitral is for payment of a sum of money, the action will take the form of a simple action for payment. In other cases a decree of specific implement in terms of the decree-arbitral will be required.

Alternatively, recourse to the court may be avoided: if the arbitration agreement contains a consent to registration of the award in the Books of Council and Session for execution and the award is so registered, the award may be enforced by summary diligence. The consent to registration must be that of the party against whom summary diligence is to proceed.

Challenge of Award

There is in Scotland no right of appeal against an award. (Contrast section 69 of the Act of 1996, conferring a right of appeal on a point of law arising out of an award.) However, in Scotland an award may be set aside by an order for reduction competent only in the Court of Session.

The limited grounds of reduction are:

- "corruption, bribery or falsehood";
- excess of jurisdiction;
- improper procedure; and
- defects in the award.

Partial reduction is competent but only where one part of the award is open to objection, the other part is valid and the two parts are clearly severable.

"Corruption, bribery or falsehood"

The phrase is quoted from the 25th Act of the Articles of Regulation of 1695. These Articles were made by Commissioners under the special sanction of an Act of the Parliament of Scotland of 1693, and the 25th of them dealt with the grounds on which an arbiter's award might be challenged. It provided:

> "That for the cutting off of groundless and expensive pleas and processes in time coming, the Lords of Session sustain no reduction of any decree-arbitral that shall be pronounced hereafter upon a subscribed submission, at the instance of either of the

parties-submitters, upon any cause or reason whatsoever, unless that of corruption, bribery, or falsehood, to be alleged against the judges-arbitrators who pronounced the same".

The provision must be viewed in its historical context. Before 1695 the courts of law had come to allow an award to be challenged in the courts on the grounds of "iniquity" by an arbiter or of "enorm lesion" suffered by a party, *i.e.* on the grounds that an arbiter had made a mistake or that a party had suffered undue hardship. The result was that in practically every case an award could be reviewed upon its merits at the discretion of the court—a situation which defeated the main object of the parties in resorting to arbitration.

The aim of the 25th Article was to end the practice of review by the court: arbiters' awards were to be final and binding on the parties and were no longer to be open to challenge merely because the arbiter had made a mistake or one party had suffered undue hardship. Corruption, bribery and falsehood on the part of the arbiter, however, were to remain grounds on which an award could be challenged in court.

If the statutory provision had been given a literal interpretation it would have prevented an award from being set aside on any ground other than corruption, bribery, or falsehood. Decided cases, however, and particularly the speech of Lord Watson in the House of Lords case *Adams v. Great North of Scotland Railway Co.* (1891), established that the object for which the provisions had been made had to be looked to: the provisions had never been intended to go beyond the point of putting an end to the practice of review upon the merits; other common law grounds of challenge (see below) remained available.

In some cases there were attempts to extend the word "corruption" so as to include "legal corruption" or "constructive corruption", *i.e.* conduct on the part of the arbiter which was mistaken but not strictly corrupt. Lord Watson in *Adams v. Great North of Scotland Railway Co.* protested against this extended meaning of "corruption"; actual corruption was necessary if an award was to be set aside on the ground of the Articles of Regulation: if the arbiter's mistake was innocent, it could not be brought within the term "corruption", though it might lead to reduction of the award on one of the other grounds mentioned below.

Excess of jurisdiction

An award which is *ultra fines compromissi* ("beyond the bounds of the submission") may be set aside.

Improper procedure

Failure to comply with the procedure specified by the parties would come under this heading, as well as failure to observe implied conditions of honesty and impartiality.

Defects in award

The award should be clear in its terms, correct in its form (*e.g.* if the arbitration was started by a formal deed of submission in probative form, the award would require to be in that form (*M'Laren v. Aikman* (1939)), include nothing which was not referred and exhaust all that was referred. It must not have been obtained by improper means such as fraud on the part of the parties, and it must have been delivered, and so be out of the control of the arbiter.

Partial reduction may be possible if good parts of the award can be separated from invalid parts.

The mere fact that an arbiter has made no finding as to expenses is not a ground for reducing the award (*Pollich v. Heatley* (1910)).

Judicial References

By a judicial reference is meant the procedure by which parties to a court action agree to withdraw the decision of the whole or some of the questions raised in the action from the decision of the court and, while still formally leaving the action in court, refer these questions to an arbiter.

A judicial reference is started by the lodging with the court (sheriff or Lord Ordinary) of a "minute" stating the agreement of the parties, and the court then, if it thinks fit, "interpones authority to the minute", *i.e.* authorises the judicial reference to proceed.

The selection of the judicial referee is a matter for the parties to decide. Like an ordinary arbiter, a judicial referee is not bound by strict court procedure.

The scope of the reference is limited to the subject-matter of the action as set out in the "record".

The decision of a judicial referee takes the form of a report to the court (not an award). The report may be challenged on the same grounds as an award in an ordinary arbitration. The court will either approve of the report and grant "decree conform", *i.e.* make a court order in conformity with the terms of the report, or set the report aside; the court has no power to amend the report.

The Model Law

Unlike England, Scotland has adopted the UNCITRAL Model Law for *international commercial* arbitration. The provisions are in sections 66 of, and Schedule 7 to, the Law Reform (Miscellaneous Provisions) (Scotland) Act 1990. Schedule 7 consists of the Model Law with some minor modifications (see Ferguson, *Arbitration*, Appendix V.).

Article 1 of the Model Law provides that an arbitration is international if:

- at the time of entering into the arbitration agreement the parties have their places of business in different states, or
- there is situated outside the state or states in which the parties have their places of business:
  - (a) the place of arbitration;
  - (b) any place where a substantial part of the obligations of their commercial relationship is to be performed; or
  - (c) the place with which the subject-matter of the dispute is most closely connected.

Article 2 defines the word "commercial" in relation to an arbitration as including matters arising from all relationships of a commercial nature, whether contractual or not.

Even where an arbitration falls outside the scope of the Model Law because it is not international within Article 1 or commercial within Article 2, the parties may agree that the Model Law is to apply to their arbitration. The Model Law is not, however, a complete code and where parties have contracted into it, their arbitration will be governed by the domestic statute and common law where the Model Law does not regulate the matter in question.

The Scottish Arbitration Code

The Scottish Arbitration Code was published in 1999 for use in domestic and international arbitration. It was prepared by the Scottish Council for International Arbitration, the Chartered Institute of Arbitrators (Scottish Branch) and the Scottish Building Contract Committee.

Introducing the Code, Lord Rodger of Earlsferry, Lord President of the Court of Session, stated:

> "Arbitration has long played an important role in settling disputes in Scotland. The Scottish courts always recognised the right of

parties to agree to exclude the jurisdiction of the courts and to refer any problems to arbitration. So, in many ways, Scotland should have been an ideal place to arbitrate. There was one drawback, however. The ancient lineage of our domestic law meant that its rules tended to be found scattered in various places—some in old cases and others in various statutes. . . .

. . . The Code sets out clearly and concisely all the provisions which would apply to an arbitration, whether domestic or international. They contain a judicious mixture of firm rules and flexibility. With the aid of the Code it should be easy for parties to devise the precise form of arbitration which best suits their needs. The preparation of the Code has inevitably involved a great deal of hard work on the part of the members of the Institute and Council. Their reward is that their members in Scotland can now offer a modern and convenient service to parties from all over the world."

Further Reading

Fraser P. Davidson, *Arbitration* (2000).

Lord Hope of Craighead on the title "Arbitration" in the *Reissue 1 of The Laws of Scotland: Stair Memorial Encyclopaedia* (1999).

Robert L.C Hunter, *The Law of Arbitration in Scotland* (1987).

Enid A Marshall, *Scots Mercantile Law* (3rd ed., 1997), Chap. 10.

Enid A Marshall, *General Principles of Scots Law* (7th ed., 1999), Chapter 2.

John Montgomerie Bell, *Treatise on the Law of Arbitration in Scotland* (2nd ed., 1877).

James Campbell Irons and R. D. Melville, *Treatise on the Law of Arbitration in Scotland* (1903.

Fraser P. Davidson, *International Commercial Law: Scotland and the UNCITRAL Model Law* (1991).

TABLE OF APPENDICES

APPENDIX 1

ARBITRATION ACT 1996

(1996 c 23)

ARRANGEMENT OF SECTIONS

PART I

ARBITRATION PURSUANT TO AN ARBITRATIAON AGREEMENT

Introductory

SECTION

The arbitration agreement

Stay of legal proceedings

Commencement of arbitral proceedings

The arbitral tribunal

Jurisdiction of the arbitral tribunal

The arbitral proceedings

Powers of court in relation to arbitral proceedings

The award

Costs of the arbitration

Powers of the court in relation to award

Miscellaneous

Supplementary

Part II

Other Provisions Relating to Arbitration

Domestic arbitration agreements

Consumer arbitration agreements

Small claims arbitration in the county court

Appointment of judges as arbitrators

Statutory arbitrations

PART III

RECOGNITION AND ENFORCEMENT OF CERTAIN FOREIGN AWARDS

Enforcement of Geneva Convention awards

Recognition and enforcement of New York Convention awards

PART IV

GENERAL PROVISIONS

SCHEDULES:

An Act to restate and improve the law relating to arbitration pursuant to an arbitration agreement; to make other provision relating to arbitration and arbitration awards; and for connected purposes.

[17th June 1996]

BE IT ENACTED by the Queen's most Excellent Majesty, by and with the advice and consent of the Lords Spiritual and Temporal, and Commons, in this present Parliament assembled, and by the authority of the same, as follows:—

Part I

Arbitration Pursuant to an Arbitration Agreement

Introductory

General principles

1.—The provisions of this Part are founded on the following principles, and shall be construed accordingly—

(a) the object of arbitration is to obtain the fair resolution of disputes by an impartial tribunal without unnecessary delay or expense;

(b) the parties should be free to agree how their disputes are resolved, subject only to such safeguards as are necessary in the public interest;

(c) in matters governed by this Part the court should not intervene except as provided by this Part.

Scope of application of provisions

2.—(1) The provisions of this Part apply where the seat of the arbitration is in England and Wales or Northern Ireland.

(2) The following sections apply even if the seat of the arbitration is outside England and Wales or Northern Ireland or no seat has been designated or determined—

(a) sections 9 to 11 (stay of legal proceedings, &c.), and

(b) section 66 (enforcement of arbitral awards).

(3) The powers conferred by the following sections apply even if the seat of the arbitration is outside England and Wales or Northern Ireland or no seat has been designated or determined—

(a) section 43 (securing the attendance of witnesses), and

(b) section 44 (court powers exercisable in support of arbitral proceedings);

but the court may refuse to exercise any such power if, in the opinion of the court, the fact that the seat of the arbitration is outside England and Wales or Northern Ireland, or that when designated or determined the seat is likely to be outside England and Wales or Northern Ireland, makes it inappropriate to do so.

(4) The court may exercise a power conferred by any provision of this Part not mentioned in subsection (2) or (3) for the purpose of supporting the arbitral process where—

(a) no seat of the arbitration has been designated or determined, and

(b) by reason of a connection with England and Wales or Northern Ireland the court is satisfied that it is appropriate to do so.

(5) Section 7 (separability of arbitration agreement) and section 8 (death of a party) apply where the law applicable to the arbitration agreement is the law of England and Wales or Northern Ireland even if the seat of the arbitration is outside England and Wales or Northern Ireland or has not been designated or determined.

The seat of the arbitration

3.—In this Part "the seat of the arbitration" means the juridical seat of the arbitration designated—

(a) by the parties to the arbitration agreement, or

(b) by any arbitral or other institution or person vested by the parties with powers in that regard, or

(c) by the arbitral tribunal if so authorised by the parties,

or determined, in the absence of any such designation, having regard to the parties' agreement and all the relevant circumstances.

Mandatory and non-mandatory provisions

4.—(1) The mandatory provisions of this Part are listed in Schedule 1 and have effect notwithstanding any agreement to the contrary.
(2) The other provisions of this Part (the "non-mandatory provisions") allow the parties to make their own arrangements by agreement but provide rules which apply in the absence of such agreement.
(3) The parties may make such arrangements by agreeing to the application of institutional rules or providing any other means by which a matter may be decided.
(4) It is immaterial whether or not the law applicable to the parties' agreement is the law of England and Wales or, as the case may be, Northern Ireland.
(5) The choice of a law other than the law of England and Wales or Northern Ireland as the applicable law in respect of a matter provided for by a non-mandatory provision of this Part is equivalent to an agreement making provision about that matter.

For this purpose an applicable law determined in accordance with the parties' agreement, or which is objectively determined in the absence of any express or implied choice, shall be treated as chosen by the parties.

Agreements to be in writing

5.—(1) The provisions of this Part apply only where the arbitration agreement is in writing, and any other agreement between the parties as to any matter is effective for the purposes of this Part only if in writing.

The expressions "agreement", "agree" and "agreed" shall be construed accordingly.

(2) There is an agreement in writing—

(a) if the agreement is made in writing (whether or not it is signed by the parties),

(b) if the agreement is made by exchange of communications in writing, or

(c) if the agreement is evidenced in writing.

(3) Where parties agree otherwise than in writing by reference to terms which are in writing, they make an agreement in writing.
(4) An agreement is evidenced in writing if an agreement made otherwise than in writing is recorded by one of the parties, or by a third party, with the authority of the parties to the agreement.
(5) An exchange of written submissions in arbitral or legal proceedings in which the existence of an agreement otherwise than in writing is alleged by one party against another party and not denied by the other party in his response constitutes as between those parties an agreement in writing to the effect alleged.
(6) References in this Part to anything being written or in writing include its being recorded by any means.

The arbitration agreement

Definition of arbitration agreement

6.—(1) In this Part an "arbitration agreement" means an agreement to submit to arbitration present or future disputes (whether they are contractual or not).
(2) The reference in an agreement to a written form of arbitration clause or to a document containing an arbitration clause constitutes an arbitration agreement if the reference is such as to make that clause part of the agreement.

Separability of arbitration agreement

7.—Unless otherwise agreed by the parties, an arbitration agreement which forms or was intended to form part of another agreement (whether or not in writing) shall not be regarded as invalid, non-existent or ineffective because that other agreement is invalid, or did not come into existence or has become ineffective, and it shall for that purpose be treated as a distinct agreement.

Whether agreement discharged by death of a party

8.—(1) Unless otherwise agreed by the parties, an arbitration agreement is not discharged by the death of a party and may be enforced by or against the personal representatives of that party.
(2) Subsection (1) does not affect the operation of any enactment or rule of law by virtue of which a substantive right or obligation is extinguished by death.

Stay of legal proceedings

9.—(1) A party to an arbitration agreement against whom legal proceedings are brought (whether by way of claim or counterclaim) in respect of a matter which under the agreement is to be referred to arbitration may (upon notice to the other parties to the proceedings) apply to the court in which the proceedings have been brought to stay the proceedings so far as they concern that matter.
(2) An application may be made notwithstanding that the matter is to be referred to arbitration only after the exhaustion of other dispute resolution procedures.
(3) An application may not be made by a person before taking the appropriate procedural step (if any) to acknowledge the legal proceedings against him or after he has taken any step in those proceedings to answer the substantive claim.
(4) On an application under this section the court shall grant a stay unless satisfied that the arbitration agreement is null and void, inoperative, or incapable of being performed.
(5) If the court refuses to stay the legal proceedings, any provision that an award is a condition precedent to the bringing of legal proceedings in respect of any matter is of no effect in relation to those proceedings.

Reference of interpleader issue to arbitration

10.—(1) Where in legal proceedings relief by way of interpleader is granted and any issue between the claimants is one in respect of which there is an arbitration agreement between them, the court granting the relief shall direct that the issue be determined in accordance with the agreement unless the circumstances are such that proceedings brought by a claimant in respect of the matter would not be stayed.
(2) Where subsection (1) applies but the court does not direct that the issue be determined in accordance with the arbitration agreement, any provision that an award is a condition precedent to the bringing of legal proceedings in respect of any matter shall not affect the determination of that issue by the court.

Retention of security where Admiralty proceedings stayed

11.—(1) Where Admiralty proceedings are stayed on the ground that the dispute in question should be submitted to arbitration, the court granting the stay may, if in those proceedings property has been arrested or bail or other security has been given to prevent or obtain release from arrest—

(a) order that the property arrested be retained as security for the satisfaction of any award given in the arbitration in respect of that dispute, or

(b) order that the stay of those proceedings be conditional on the provision of equivalent security for the satisfaction of any such award.

(2) Subject to any provision made by rules of court and to any necessary modifications, the same law and practice shall apply in relation to property retained in pursuance of an order as would apply if it were held for the purposes of proceedings in the court making the order.

Commencement of arbitral proceedings

Power of court to extend time for beginning arbitral proceedings, &c

12.—(1) Where an arbitration agreement to refer future disputes to arbitration provides that a claim shall be barred, or the claimant's right extinguished, unless the claimant takes within a time fixed by the agreement some step—

(a) to begin arbitral proceedings, or

(b) to begin other dispute resolution procedures which must be exhausted before arbitral proceedings can be begun,

the court may by order extend the time for taking that step.

(2) Any party to the arbitration agreement may apply for such an order (upon notice to the other parties), but only after a claim has arisen and after exhausting any available arbitral process for obtaining an extension of time.

(3) The court shall make an order only if satisfied—

(a) that the circumstances are such as were outside the reasonable contemplation of the parties when they agreed the provision in question, and that it would be just to extend the time, or

(b) that the conduct of one party makes it unjust to hold the other party to the strict terms of the provision in question.

(4) The court may extend the time for such period and on such terms as it thinks fit, and may do so whether or not the time previously fixed (by agreement or by a previous order) has expired.

(5) An order under this section does not affect the operation of the Limitation Acts (see section 13).

(6) The leave of the court is required for any appeal from a decision of the court under this section.

Application of Limitation Acts

13.—(1) The Limitation Acts apply to arbitral proceedings as they apply to legal proceedings.

(2) The court may order that in computing the time prescribed by the Limitation Acts for the commencement of proceedings (including arbitral proceedings) in respect of a dispute which was the subject matter—

(a) of an award which the court orders to be set aside or declares to be of no effect, or

(b) of the affected part of an award which the court orders to be set aside in part, or declares to be in part of no effect,

the period between the commencement of the arbitration and the date of the order referred to in paragraph (a) or (b) shall be excluded.

(3) In determining for the purposes of the Limitation Acts when a cause of action accrued, any provision that an award is a condition precedent to the bringing of legal proceedings in respect of a matter to which an arbitration agreement applies shall be disregarded.

(4) In this Part "the Limitation Acts" means—

(a) in England and Wales, the Limitation Act 1980, the Foreign Limitation Periods Act 1984 and any other enactment (whenever passed) relating to the limitation of actions;

(b) in Northern Ireland, the Limitation (Northern Ireland) Order 1989, the Foreign Limitation Periods (Northern Ireland) Order 1985 and any other enactment (whenever passed) relating to the limitation of actions.

Commencement of arbitral proceedings

14.—(1) The parties are free to agree when arbitral proceedings are to be regarded as commenced for the purposes of this Part and for the purposes of the Limitation Acts.

(2) If there is no such agreement the following provisions apply.

(3) Where the arbitrator is named or designated in the arbitration agreement, arbitral proceedings are commenced in respect of a matter when one party serves on the other party or parties a notice in writing requiring him or them to submit that matter to the person so named or designated.

(4) Where the arbitrator or arbitrators are to be appointed by the parties, arbitral proceedings are commenced in respect of a matter when one party serves on the other party or parties notice in writing requiring him or them to appoint an arbitrator or to agree to the appointment of an arbitrator in respect of that matter.

(5) Where the arbitrator or arbitrators are to be appointed by a person other than a party to the proceedings, arbitral proceedings are commenced in respect of a matter when one party gives notice in writing to that person requesting him to make the appointment in respect of that matter.

The arbitral tribunal

The arbitral tribunal

15.— (1) The parties are free to agree on the number of arbitrators to form the tribunal and whether there is to be a chairman or umpire.

(2) Unless otherwise agreed by the parties, an agreement that the number of arbitrators shall be two or any other even number shall be understood as requiring the appointment of an additional arbitrator as chairman of the tribunal.

(3) If there is no agreement as to the number of arbitrators, the tribunal shall consist of a sole arbitrator.

Procedure for appointment of arbitrators

16.—(1) The parties are free to agree on the procedure for appointing the arbitrator or arbitrators, including the procedure for appointing any chairman or umpire.
(2) If or to the extent that there is no such agreement, the following provisions apply.
(3) If the tribunal is to consist of a sole arbitrator, the parties shall jointly appoint the arbitrator not later than 28 days after service of a request in writing by either party to do so.
(4) If the tribunal is to consist of two arbitrators, each party shall appoint one arbitrator not later than 14 days after service of a request in writing by either party to do so.
(5) If the tribunal is to consist of three arbitrators—

(a) each party shall appoint one arbitrator not later than 14 days after service of a request in writing by either party to do so, and

(b) the two so appointed shall forthwith appoint a third arbitrator as the chairman of the tribunal.

(6) If the tribunal is to consist of two arbitrators and an umpire—

(a) each party shall appoint one arbitrator not later than 14 days after service of a request in writing by either party to do so, and

(b) the two so appointed may appoint an umpire at any time after they themselves are appointed and shall do so before any substantive hearing or forthwith if they cannot agree on a matter relating to the arbitration.

(7) In any other case (in particular, if there are more than two parties) section 18 applies as in the case of a failure of the agreed appointment procedure.

Power in case of default to appoint sole arbitrator

17.—(1) Unless the parties otherwise agree, where each of two parties to an arbitration agreement is to appoint an arbitrator and one party ("the party in default") refuses to do so, or fails to do so within the time specified, the other party, having duly appointed his arbitrator, may give notice in writing to the party in default that he proposes to appoint his arbitrator to act as sole arbitrator.
(2) If the party in default does not within 7 clear days of that notice being given—

(a) make the required appointment, and

(b) notify the other party that he has done so,

the other party may appoint his arbitrator as sole arbitrator whose award shall be binding on both parties as if he had been so appointed by agreement.

(3) Where a sole arbitrator has been appointed under subsection (2), the party in default may (upon notice to the appointing party) apply to the court which may set aside the appointment.

(4) The leave of the court is required for any appeal from a decision of the court under this section.

Failure of appointment procedure

18.—(1) The parties are free to agree what is to happen in the event of a failure of the procedure for the appointment of the arbitral tribunal.

There is no failure if an appointment is duly made under section 17 (power in case of default to appoint sole arbitrator), unless that appointment is set aside.

(2) If or to the extent that there is no such agreement any party to the arbitration agreement may (upon notice to the other parties) apply to the court to exercise its powers under this section.

(3) Those powers are—

(a) to give directions as to the making of any necessary appointments;

(b) to direct that the tribunal shall be constituted by such appointments (or any one or more of them) as have been made;

(c) to revoke any appointments already made;

(d) to make any necessary appointments itself.

(4) An appointment made by the court under this section has effect as if made with the agreement of the parties.

(5) The leave of the court is required for any appeal from a decision of the court under this section.

Court to have regard to agreed qualifications

19.—In deciding whether to exercise, and in considering how to exercise, any of its powers under section 16 (procedure for appointment of arbitrators) or section 18 (failure of appointment procedure), the court shall have due regard to any agreement of the parties as to the qualifications required of the arbitrators.

Chairman

20.—(1) Where the parties have agreed that there is to be a chairman, they are free to agree what the functions of the chairman are to be in relation to the making of decisions, orders and awards.

(2) If or to the extent that there is no such agreement, the following provisions apply.

(3) Decisions, orders and awards shall be made by all or a majority of the arbitrators (including the chairman).

(4) The view of the chairman shall prevail in relation to a decision, order or award in respect of which there is neither unanimity nor a majority under subsection (3).

Umpire

21.—(1) Where the parties have agreed that there is to be an umpire, they are free to agree what the functions of the umpire are to be, and in particular—

(a) whether he is to attend the proceedings, and

(b) when he is to replace the other arbitrators as the tribunal with power to make decisions, orders and awards.

(2) If or to the extent that there is no such agreement, the following provisions apply.
(3) The umpire shall attend the proceedings and be supplied with the same documents and other materials as are supplied to the other arbitrators.
(4) Decisions, orders and awards shall be made by the other arbitrators unless and until they cannot agree on a matter relating to the arbitration.
In that event they shall forthwith give notice in writing to the parties and the umpire, whereupon the umpire shall replace them as the tribunal with power to make decisions, orders and awards as if he were sole arbitrator.
(5) If the arbitrators cannot agree but fail to give notice of that fact, or if any of them fails to join in the giving of notice, any party to the arbitral proceedings may (upon notice to the other parties and to the tribunal) apply to the court which may order that the umpire shall replace the other arbitrators as the tribunal with power to make decisions, orders and awards as if he were sole arbitrator.
(6) The leave of the court is required for any appeal from a decision of the court under this section.

Decision-making where no chairman or umpire

22.—(1) Where the parties agree that there shall be two or more arbitrators with no chairman or umpire, the parties are free to agree how the tribunal is to make decisions, orders and awards.
(2) If there is no such agreement, decisions, orders and awards shall be made by all or a majority of the arbitrators.

Revocation of arbitrator's authority

23.—(1) The parties are free to agree in what circumstances the authority of an arbitrator may be revoked.
(2) If or to the extent that there is no such agreement the following provisions apply.
(3) The authority of an arbitrator may not be revoked except—

(a) by the parties acting jointly, or

(b) by an arbitral or other institution or person vested by the parties with powers in that regard.

(4) Revocation of the authority of an arbitrator by the parties acting jointly must be agreed in writing unless the parties also agree (whether or not in writing) to terminate the arbitration agreement.
(5) Nothing in this section affects the power of the court—

(a) to revoke an appointment under section 18 (powers exercisable in case of failure of appointment procedure), or

(b) to remove an arbitrator on the grounds specified in section 24.

Power of court to remove arbitrator

24.—(1) A party to arbitral proceedings may (upon notice to the other parties, to the arbitrator concerned and to any other arbitrator) apply to the court to remove an arbitrator on any of the following grounds—

(a) that circumstances exist that give rise to justifiable doubts as to his impartiality;

(b) that he does not possess the qualifications required by the arbitration agreement;

(c) that he is physically or mentally incapable of conducting the proceedings or there are justifiable doubts as to his capacity to do so;

(d) that he has refused or failed—

(i) properly to conduct the proceedings, or
(ii) to use all reasonable despatch in conducting the proceedings or making an award,

and that substantial injustice has been or will be caused to the applicant.

(2) If there is an arbitral or other institution or person vested by the parties with power to remove an arbitrator, the court shall not exercise its power of removal unless satisfied that the applicant has first exhausted any available recourse to that institution or person.
(3) The arbitral tribunal may continue the arbitral proceedings and make an award while an application to the court under this section is pending.
(4) Where the court removes an arbitrator, it may make such order as it thinks fit with respect to his entitlement (if any) to fees or expenses, or the repayment of any fees or expenses already paid.
(5) The arbitrator concerned is entitled to appear and be heard by the court before it makes any order under this section.
(6) The leave of the court is required for any appeal from a decision of the court under this section.

Resignation of arbitrator

25.—(1) The parties are free to agree with an arbitrator as to the consequences of his resignation as regards—

(a) his entitlement (if any) to fees or expenses, and

(b) any liability thereby incurred by him.

(2) If or to the extent that there is no such agreement the following provisions apply.
(3) An arbitrator who resigns his appointment may (upon notice to the parties) apply to the court—

(a) to grant him relief from any liability thereby incurred by him, and

(b) to make such order as it thinks fit with respect to his entitlement (if any) to fees or expenses or the repayment of any fees or expenses already paid.

(4) If the court is satisfied that in all the circumstances it was reasonable for the arbitrator to resign, it may grant such relief as is mentioned in subsection (3)(a) on such terms as it thinks fit.
(5) The leave of the court is required for any appeal from a decision of the court under this section.

Death of arbitrator or person appointing him

26.—(1) The authority of an arbitrator is personal and ceases on his death.
(2) Unless otherwise agreed by the parties, the death of the person by whom an arbitrator was appointed does not revoke the arbitrator's authority.

Filling of vacancy, &c

27.—(1) Where an arbitrator ceases to hold office, the parties are free to agree—

(a) whether and if so how the vacancy is to be filled,

(b) whether and if so to what extent the previous proceedings should stand, and

(c) what effect (if any) his ceasing to hold office has on any appointment made by him (alone or jointly).

(2) If or to the extent that there is no such agreement, the following provisions apply.
(3) The provisions of sections 16 (procedure for appointment of arbitrators) and 18 (failure of appointment procedure) apply in relation to the filling of the vacancy as in relation to an original appointment.
(4) The tribunal (when reconstituted) shall determine whether and if so to what extent the previous proceedings should stand.

This does not affect any right of a party to challenge those proceedings on any ground which had arisen before the arbitrator ceased to hold office.
(5) His ceasing to hold office does not affect any appointment by him (alone or jointly) of another arbitrator, in particular any appointment of a chairman or umpire.

Joint and several liability of parties to arbitrators for fees and expenses

28.—(1) The parties are jointly and severally liable to pay to the arbitrators such reasonable fees and expenses (if any) as are appropriate in the circumstances.
(2) Any party may apply to the court (upon notice to the other parties and to the arbitrators) which may order that the amount of the arbitrators' fees and expenses shall be considered and adjusted by such means and upon such terms as it may direct.
(3) If the application is made after any amount has been paid to the arbitrators by way of fees or expenses, the court may order the repayment of such amount (if any) as is shown to be excessive, but shall not do so unless it is shown that it is reasonable in the circumstances to order repayment.
(4) The above provisions have effect subject to any order of the court under section 24(4) or 25(3)(b) (order as to entitlement to fees or expenses in case of removal or resignation of arbitrator).
(5) Nothing in this section affects any liability of a party to any other party to pay all or any of the costs of the arbitration (see sections 59 to 65) or any contractual right of an arbitrator to payment of his fees and expenses.
(6) In this section references to arbitrators include an arbitrator who has ceased to act and an umpire who has not replaced the other arbitrators.

Immunity of arbitrator

29.—(1) An arbitrator is not liable for anything done or omitted in the discharge or purported discharge of his functions as arbitrator unless the act or omission is shown to have been in bad faith.
(2) Subsection (1) applies to an employee or agent of an arbitrator as it applies to the arbitrator himself.
(3) This section does not affect any liability incurred by an arbitrator by reason of his resigning (but see section 25).

Jurisdiction of the arbitral tribunal

Competence of tribunal to rule on its own jurisdiction

30.—(1) Unless otherwise agreed by the parties, the arbitral tribunal may rule on its own substantive jurisdiction, that is, as to—

(a) whether there is a valid arbitration agreement,

(b) whether the tribunal is properly constituted, and

(c) what matters have been submitted to arbitration in accordance with the arbitration agreement.

(2) Any such ruling may be challenged by any available arbitral process of appeal or review or in accordance with the provisions of this Part.

Objection to substantive jurisdiction of tribunal

31.—(1) An objection that the arbitral tribunal lacks substantive jurisdiction at the outset of the proceedings must be raised by a party not later than the time he takes the first step in the proceedings to contest the merits of any matter in relation to which he challenges the tribunal's jurisdiction.
A party is not precluded from raising such an objection by the fact that he has appointed or participated in the appointment of an arbitrator.
(2) Any objection during the course of the arbitral proceedings that the arbitral tribunal is exceeding its substantive jurisdiction must be made as soon as possible after the matter alleged to be beyond its jurisdiction is raised.
(3) The arbitral tribunal may admit an objection later than the time specified in subsection (1) or (2) if it considers the delay justified.
(4) Where an objection is duly taken to the tribunal's substantive jurisdiction and the tribunal has power to rule on its own jurisdiction, it may—

(a) rule on the matter in an award as to jurisdiction, or

(b) deal with the objection in its award on the merits.

If the parties agree which of these courses the tribunal should take, the tribunal shall proceed accordingly.
(5) The tribunal may in any case, and shall if the parties so agree, stay proceedings whilst an application is made to the court under section 32 (determination of preliminary point of jurisdiction).

Determination of preliminary point of jurisdiction

32.—(1) The court may, on the application of a party to arbitral proceedings (upon notice to the other parties), determine any question as to the substantive jurisdiction of the tribunal.
A party may lose the right to object (see section 73).
(2) An application under this section shall not be considered unless—

(a) it is made with the agreement in writing of all the other parties to the proceedings, or

(b) it is made with the permission of the tribunal and the court is satisfied—

(i) that the determination of the question is likely to produce substantial savings in costs,
(ii) that the application was made without delay, and
(iii) that there is good reason why the matter should be decided by the court.

(3) An application under this section, unless made with the agreement of all the other parties to the proceedings, shall state the grounds on which it is said that the matter should be decided by the court.

(4) Unless otherwise agreed by the parties, the arbitral tribunal may continue the arbitral proceedings and make an award while an application to the court under this section is pending.
(5) Unless the court gives leave, no appeal lies from a decision of the court whether the conditions specified in subsection (2) are met.
(6) The decision of the court on the question of jurisdiction shall be treated as a judgment of the court for the purposes of an appeal.
But no appeal lies without the leave of the court which shall not be given unless the court considers that the question involves a point of law which is one of general importance or is one which for some other special reason should be considered by the Court of Appeal.

The arbitral proceedings

General duty of the tribunal

33.—(1) The tribunal shall—

(a) act fairly and impartially as between the parties, giving each party a reasonable opportunity of putting his case and dealing with that of his opponent, and

(b) adopt procedures suitable to the circumstances of the particular case, avoiding unnecessary delay or expense, so as to provide a fair means for the resolution of the matters falling to be determined.

(2) The tribunal shall comply with that general duty in conducting the arbitral proceedings, in its decisions on matters of procedure and evidence and in the exercise of all other powers conferred on it.

Procedural and evidential matters

34.—(1) It shall be for the tribunal to decide all procedural and evidential matters, subject to the right of the parties to agree any matter.
(2) Procedural and evidential matters include—

(a) when and where any part of the proceedings is to be held;

(b) the language or languages to be used in the proceedings and whether translations of any relevant documents are to be supplied;

(c) whether any and if so what form of written statements of claim and defence are to be used, when these should be supplied and the extent to which such statements can be later amended;

(d) whether any and if so which documents or classes of documents should be disclosed between and produced by the parties and at what stage;

(e) whether any and if so what questions should be put to and answered by the respective parties and when and in what form this should be done;

(f) whether to apply strict rules of evidence (or any other rules) as to the admissibility, relevance or weight of any material (oral, written or other) sought to be tendered on any matters of fact or opinion, and the time, manner and form in which such material should be exchanged and presented;

(g) whether and to what extent the tribunal should itself take the initiative in ascertaining the facts and the law;

(h) whether and to what extent there should be oral or written evidence or submissions.

(3) The tribunal may fix the time within which any directions given by it are to be complied with, and may if it thinks fit extend the time so fixed (whether or not it has expired).

Consolidation of proceedings and concurrent hearings

35.—(1) The parties are free to agree—

(a) that the arbitral proceedings shall be consolidated with other arbitral proceedings, or

(b) that concurrent hearings shall be held,

on such terms as may be agreed.

(2) Unless the parties agree to confer such power on the tribunal, the tribunal has no power to order consolidation of proceedings or concurrent hearings.

Legal or other representation

36.—Unless otherwise agreed by the parties, a party to arbitral proceedings may be represented in the proceedings by a lawyer or other person chosen by him.

Power to appoint experts, legal advisers or assessors

37.—(1) Unless otherwise agreed by the parties—

(a) the tribunal may—

(i) appoint experts or legal advisers to report to it and the parties, or

(ii) appoint assessors to assist it on technical matters, and may allow any such expert, legal adviser or assessor to attend the proceedings; and

(b) the parties shall be given a reasonable opportunity to comment on any information, opinion or advice offered by any such person.

(2) The fees and expenses of an expert, legal adviser or assessor appointed by the tribunal for which the arbitrators are liable are expenses of the arbitrators for the purposes of this Part.

General powers exercisable by the tribunal

38.—(1) The parties are free to agree on the powers exercisable by the arbitral tribunal for the purposes of and in relation to the proceedings.
(2) Unless otherwise agreed by the parties the tribunal has the following powers.
(3) The tribunal may order a claimant to provide security for the costs of the arbitration.
This power shall not be exercised on the ground that the claimant is—

(a) an individual ordinarily resident outside the United Kingdom, or

(b) a corporation or association incorporated or formed under the law of a country outside the United Kingdom, or whose central management and control is exercised outside the United Kingdom.

(4) The tribunal may give directions in relation to any property which is the subject of the proceedings or as to which any question arises in the proceedings, and which is owned by or is in the possession of a party to the proceedings—

(a) for the inspection, photographing, preservation, custody or detention of the property by the tribunal, an expert or a party, or

(b) ordering that samples be taken from, or any observation be made of or experiment conducted upon, the property.

(5) The tribunal may direct that a party or witness shall be examined on oath or affirmation, and may for that purpose administer any necessary oath or take any necessary affirmation.
(6) The tribunal may give directions to a party for the preservation for the purposes of the proceedings of any evidence in his custody or control.

Power to make provisional awards

39.—(1) The parties are free to agree that the tribunal shall have power to order on a provisional basis any relief which it would have power to grant in a final award.
(2) This includes, for instance, making—

(a) a provisional order for the payment of money or the disposition of property as between the parties, or

(b) an order to make an interim payment on account of the costs of the arbitration.

(3) Any such order shall be subject to the tribunal's final adjudication; and the tribunal's final award, on the merits or as to costs, shall take account of any such order.
(4) Unless the parties agree to confer such power on the tribunal, the tribunal has no such power.

This does not affect its powers under section 47 (awards on different issues, &c.).

General duty of parties

40.—(1) The parties shall do all things necessary for the proper and expeditious conduct of the arbitral proceedings.
(2) This includes—

(a) complying without delay with any determination of the tribunal as to procedural or evidential matters, or with any order or directions of the tribunal, and

(b) where appropriate, taking without delay any necessary steps to obtain a decision of the court on a preliminary question of jurisdiction or law (see sections 32 and 45).

Powers of tribunal in case of party's default

41.—(1) The parties are free to agree on the powers of the tribunal in case of a party's failure to do something necessary for the proper and expeditious conduct of the arbitration.
(2) Unless otherwise agreed by the parties, the following provisions apply.
(3) If the tribunal is satisfied that there has been inordinate and inexcusable delay on the part of the claimant in pursuing his claim and that the delay—

(a) gives rise, or is likely to give rise, to a substantial risk that it is not possible to have a fair resolution of the issues in that claim, or

(b) has caused, or is likely to cause, serious prejudice to the respondent,

the tribunal may make an award dismissing the claim.
(4) If without showing sufficient cause a party—

(a) fails to attend or be represented at an oral hearing of which due notice was given, or

(b) where matters are to be dealt with in writing, fails after due notice to submit written evidence or make written submissions,

the tribunal may continue the proceedings in the absence of that party or, as the case may be, without any written evidence or submissions on his behalf, and may make an award on the basis of the evidence before it.
(5) If without showing sufficient cause a party fails to comply with any order or directions of the tribunal, the tribunal may make a peremptory order to the same effect, prescribing such time for compliance with it as the tribunal considers appropriate.
(6) If a claimant fails to comply with a peremptory order of the tribunal to provide security for costs, the tribunal may make an award dismissing his claim.

(7) If a party fails to comply with any other kind of peremptory order, then, without prejudice to section 42 (enforcement by court of tribunal's peremptory orders), the tribunal may do any of the following—

(a) direct that the party in default shall not be entitled to rely upon any allegation or material which was the subject matter of the order;

(b) draw such adverse inferences from the act of non-compliance as the circumstances justify;

(c) proceed to an award on the basis of such materials as have been properly provided to it;

(d) make such order as it thinks fit as to the payment of costs of the arbitration incurred in consequence of the non-compliance.

Powers of court in relation to arbitral proceedings

Enforcement of peremptory orders of tribunal

42.—(1) Unless otherwise agreed by the parties, the court may make an order requiring a party to comply with a peremptory order made by the tribunal.
(2) An application for an order under this section may be made—

(a) by the tribunal (upon notice to the parties),

(b) by a party to the arbitral proceedings with the permission of the tribunal (and upon notice to the other parties), or

(c) where the parties have agreed that the powers of the court under this section shall be available.

(3) The court shall not act unless it is satisfied that the applicant has exhausted any available arbitral process in respect of failure to comply with the tribunal's order.
(4) No order shall be made under this section unless the court is satisfied that the person to whom the tribunal's order was directed has failed to comply with it within the time prescribed in the order or, if no time was prescribed, within a reasonable time.
(5) The leave of the court is required for any appeal from a decision of the court under this section.

Securing the attendance of witnesses

43.—(1) A party to arbitral proceedings may use the same court procedures as are available in relation to legal proceedings to secure the attendance before the tribunal of a witness in order to give oral testimony or to produce documents or other material evidence.
(2) This may only be done with the permission of the tribunal or the agreement of the other parties.
(3) The court procedures may only be used if—

(a) the witness is in the United Kingdom, and

(b) the arbitral proceedings are being conducted in England and Wales or, as the case may be, Northern Ireland.

(4) A person shall not be compelled by virtue of this section to produce any document or other material evidence which he could not be compelled to produce in legal proceedings.

Court powers exercisable in support of arbitral proceedings

44.—(1) Unless otherwise agreed by the parties, the court has for the purposes of and in relation to arbitral proceedings the same power of making orders about the matters listed below as it has for the purposes of and in relation to legal proceedings.
(2) Those matters are—

(a) the taking of the evidence of witnesses;

(b) the preservation of evidence;

(c) making orders relating to property which is the subject of the proceedings or as to which any question arises in the proceedings—

(i) for the inspection, photographing, preservation, custody or detention of the property, or
(ii) ordering that samples be taken from, or any observation be made of or experiment conducted upon, the property;

and for that purpose authorising any person to enter any premises in the possession or control of a party to the arbitration;

(d) the sale of any goods the subject of the proceedings;

(e) the granting of an interim injunction or the appointment of a receiver.

(3) If the case is one of urgency, the court may, on the application of a party or proposed party to the arbitral proceedings, make such orders as it thinks necessary for the purpose of preserving evidence or assets.
(4) If the case is not one of urgency, the court shall act only on the application of a party to the arbitral proceedings (upon notice to the other parties and to the tribunal) made with the permission of the tribunal or the agreement in writing of the other parties.
(5) In any case the court shall act only if or to the extent that the arbitral tribunal, and any arbitral or other institution or person vested by the parties with power in that regard, has no power or is unable for the time being to act effectively.
(6) If the court so orders, an order made by it under this section shall cease to have effect in whole or in part on the order of the tribunal or of any such arbitral or other institution or person having power to act in relation to the subject-matter of the order.
(7) The leave of the court is required for any appeal from a decision of the court under this section.

Determination of preliminary point of law

45.—(1) Unless otherwise agreed by the parties, the court may on the application of a party to arbitral proceedings (upon notice to the other parties) determine any question of law arising in the course of the proceedings which the court is satisfied substantially affects the rights of one or more of the parties.
An agreement to dispense with reasons for the tribunal's award shall be considered an agreement to exclude the court's jurisdiction under this section.
(2) An application under this section shall not be considered unless—

(a) it is made with the agreement of all the other parties to the proceedings, or

(b) it is made with the permission of the tribunal and the court is satisfied—

(i) that the determination of the question is likely to produce substantial savings in costs, and
(ii) that the application was made without delay.

(3) The application shall identify the question of law to be determined and, unless made with the agreement of all the other parties to the proceedings, shall state the grounds on which it is said that the question should be decided by the court.
(4) Unless otherwise agreed by the parties, the arbitral tribunal may continue the arbitral proceedings and make an award while an application to the court under this section is pending.
(5) Unless the court gives leave, no appeal lies from a decision of the court whether the conditions specified in subsection (2) are met.
(6) The decision of the court on the question of law shall be treated as a judgment of the court for the purposes of an appeal.
But no appeal lies without the leave of the court which shall not be given unless the court considers that the question is one of general importance, or is one which for some other special reason should be considered by the Court of Appeal.

The award

Rules applicable to substance of dispute

46.—(1) The arbitral tribunal shall decide the dispute—

(a) in accordance with the law chosen by the parties as applicable to the substance of the dispute, or

(b) if the parties so agree, in accordance with such other considerations as are agreed by them or determined by the tribunal.

(2) For this purpose the choice of the laws of a country shall be understood to refer to the substantive laws of that country and not its conflict of laws rules.

(3) If or to the extent that there is no such choice or agreement, the tribunal shall apply the law determined by the conflict of laws rules which it considers applicable.

Awards on different issues, &c

47.— (1) Unless otherwise agreed by the parties, the tribunal may make more than one award at different times on different aspects of the matters to be determined.
(2) The tribunal may, in particular, make an award relating—

(a) to an issue affecting the whole claim, or

(b) to a part only of the claims or cross-claims submitted to it for decision.

(3) If the tribunal does so, it shall specify in its award the issue, or the claim or part of a claim, which is the subject matter of the award.

Remedies

48.—(1) The parties are free to agree on the powers exercisable by the arbitral tribunal as regards remedies.
(2) Unless otherwise agreed by the parties, the tribunal has the following powers.
(3) The tribunal may make a declaration as to any matter to be determined in the proceedings.
(4) The tribunal may order the payment of a sum of money, in any currency.
(5) The tribunal has the same powers as the court—

(a) to order a party to do or refrain from doing anything;

(b) to order specific performance of a contract (other than a contract relating to land);

(c) to order the rectification, setting aside or cancellation of a deed or other document.

Interest

49.—(1) The parties are free to agree on the powers of the tribunal as regards the award of interest.
(2) Unless otherwise agreed by the parties the following provisions apply.
(3) The tribunal may award simple or compound interest from such dates, at such rates and with such rests as it considers meets the justice of the case—

(a) on the whole or part of any amount awarded by the tribunal, in respect of any period up to the date of the award;

(b) on the whole or part of any amount claimed in the arbitration and outstanding at the commencement of the arbitral proceedings but paid before the award was made, in respect of any period up to the date of payment.

(4) The tribunal may award simple or compound interest from the date of the award (or any later date) until payment, at such rates and with such rests as it considers meets the justice of the case, on the outstanding amount of any award (including any award of interest under subsection (3) and any award as to costs).
(5) References in this section to an amount awarded by the tribunal include an amount payable in consequence of a declaratory award by the tribunal.
(6) The above provisions do not affect any other power of the tribunal to award interest.

Extension of time for making award

50.—(1) Where the time for making an award is limited by or in pursuance of the arbitration agreement, then, unless otherwise agreed by the parties, the court may in accordance with the following provisions by order extend that time.
(2) An application for an order under this section may be made—

(a) by the tribunal (upon notice to the parties), or

(b) by any party to the proceedings (upon notice to the tribunal and the other parties),

but only after exhausting any available arbitral process for obtaining an extension of time.
(3) The court shall only make an order if satisfied that a substantial injustice would otherwise be done.
(4) The court may extend the time for such period and on such terms as it thinks fit, and may do so whether or not the time previously fixed (by or under the agreement or by a previous order) has expired.
(5) The leave of the court is required for any appeal from a decision of the court under this section.

Settlement

51.—(1) If during arbitral proceedings the parties settle the dispute, the following provisions apply unless otherwise agreed by the parties.
(2) The tribunal shall terminate the substantive proceedings and, if so requested by the parties and not objected to by the tribunal, shall record the settlement in the form of an agreed award.
(3) An agreed award shall state that it is an award of the tribunal and shall have the same status and effect as any other award on the merits of the case.
(4) The following provisions of this Part relating to awards (sections 52 to 58) apply to an agreed award.
(5) Unless the parties have also settled the matter of the payment of the costs of the arbitration, the provisions of this Part relating to costs (sections 59 to 65) continue to apply.

Form of award

52.—(1) The parties are free to agree on the form of an award.
(2) If or to the extent that there is no such agreement, the following provisions apply.
(3) The award shall be in writing signed by all the arbitrators or all those assenting to the award.
(4) The award shall contain the reasons for the award unless it is an agreed award or the parties have agreed to dispense with reasons.
(5) The award shall state the seat of the arbitration and the date when the award is made.

Place where award treated as made

53.—Unless otherwise agreed by the parties, where the seat of the arbitration is in England and Wales or Northern Ireland, any award in the proceedings shall be treated as made there, regardless of where it was signed, despatched or delivered to any of the parties.

Date of award

54.—(1) Unless otherwise agreed by the parties, the tribunal may decide what is to be taken to be the date on which the award was made.
(2) In the absence of any such decision, the date of the award shall be taken to be the date on which it is signed by the arbitrator or, where more than one arbitrator signs the award, by the last of them.

Notification of award

55.—(1) The parties are free to agree on the requirements as to notification of the award to the parties.
(2) If there is no such agreement, the award shall be notified to the parties by service on them of copies of the award, which shall be done without delay after the award is made.
(3) Nothing in this section affects section 56 (power to withhold award in case of non-payment).

Power to withhold award in case of non-payment

56.—(1) The tribunal may refuse to deliver an award to the parties except upon full payment of the fees and expenses of the arbitrators.
(2) If the tribunal refuses on that ground to deliver an award, a party to the arbitral proceedings may (upon notice to the other parties and the tribunal) apply to the court, which may order that—

(a) the tribunal shall deliver the award on the payment into court by the applicant of the fees and expenses demanded, or such lesser amount as the court may specify,

(b) the amount of the fees and expenses properly payable shall be determined by such means and upon such terms as the court may direct, and

(c) out of the money paid into court there shall be paid out such fees and expenses as may be found to be properly payable and the balance of the money (if any) shall be paid out to the applicant.

(3) For this purpose the amount of fees and expenses properly payable is the amount the applicant is liable to pay under section 28 or any agreement relating to the payment of the arbitrators.
(4) No application to the court may be made where there is any available arbitral process for appeal or review of the amount of the fees or expenses demanded.
(5) References in this section to arbitrators include an arbitrator who has ceased to act and an umpire who has not replaced the other arbitrators.
(6) The above provisions of this section also apply in relation to any arbitral or other institution or person vested by the parties with powers in relation to the delivery of the tribunal's award.
As they so apply, the references to the fees and expenses of the arbitrators shall be construed as including the fees and expenses of that institution or person.
(7) The leave of the court is required for any appeal from a decision of the court under this section.
(8) Nothing in this section shall be construed as excluding an application under section 28 where payment has been made to the arbitrators in order to obtain the award.

Correction of award or additional award

57.—(1) The parties are free to agree on the powers of the tribunal to correct an award or make an additional award.
(2) If or to the extent there is no such agreement, the following provisions apply.
(3) The tribunal may on its own initiative or on the application of a party—

(a) correct an award so as to remove any clerical mistake or error arising from an accidental slip or omission or clarify or remove any ambiguity in the award, or

(b) make an additional award in respect of any claim (including a claim for interest or costs) which was presented to the tribunal but was not dealt with in the award.

These powers shall not be exercised without first affording the other parties a reasonable opportunity to make representations to the tribunal.
(4) Any application for the exercise of those powers must be made within 28 days of the date of the award or such longer period as the parties may agree.
(5) Any correction of an award shall be made within 28 days of the date the application was received by the tribunal or, where the correction is made by the tribunal on its own initiative, within 28 days of the date of the award or, in either case, such longer period as the parties may agree.

(6) Any additional award shall be made within 56 days of the date of the original award or such longer period as the parties may agree.
(7) Any correction of an award shall form part of the award.

Effect of award

58.—(1) Unless otherwise agreed by the parties, an award made by the tribunal pursuant to an arbitration agreement is final and binding both on the parties and on any persons claiming through or under them.
(2) This does not affect the right of a person to challenge the award by any available arbitral process of appeal or review or in accordance with the provisions of this Part.

Costs of the arbitration

Costs of the arbitration

59.—(1) References in this Part to the costs of the arbitration are to—

(a) the arbitrators' fees and expenses,
(b) the fees and expenses of any arbitral institution concerned, and
(c) the legal or other costs of the parties.

(2) Any such reference includes the costs of or incidental to any proceedings to determine the amount of the recoverable costs of the arbitration (see section 63).

Agreement to pay costs in any event

60.—An agreement which has the effect that a party is to pay the whole or part of the costs of the arbitration in any event is only valid if made after the dispute in question has arisen.

Award of costs

61.—(1) The tribunal may make an award allocating the costs of the arbitration as between the parties, subject to any agreement of the parties.
(2) Unless the parties otherwise agree, the tribunal shall award costs on the general principle that costs should follow the event except where it appears to the tribunal that in the circumstances this is not appropriate in relation to the whole or part of the costs.

Effect of agreement or award about costs

62.—Unless the parties otherwise agree, any obligation under an agreement between them as to how the costs of the arbitration are to be borne, or under an award allocating the costs of the arbitration, extends only to such costs as are recoverable.

The recoverable costs of the arbitration

63.—(1) The parties are free to agree what costs of the arbitration are recoverable.
(2) If or to the extent there is no such agreement, the following provisions apply.
(3) The tribunal may determine by award the recoverable costs of the arbitration on such basis as it thinks fit.
If it does so, it shall specify—

(a) the basis on which it has acted, and

(b) the items of recoverable costs and the amount referable to each.

(4) If the tribunal does not determine the recoverable costs of the arbitration, any party to the arbitral proceedings may apply to the court (upon notice to the other parties) which may—

(a) determine the recoverable costs of the arbitration on such basis as it thinks fit, or

(b) order that they shall be determined by such means and upon such terms as it may specify.

(5) Unless the tribunal or the court determines otherwise—

(a) the recoverable costs of the arbitration shall be determined on the basis that there shall be allowed a reasonable amount in respect of all costs reasonably incurred, and

(b) any doubt as to whether costs were reasonably incurred or were reasonable in amount shall be resolved in favour of the paying party.

(6) The above provisions have effect subject to section 64 (recoverable fees and expenses of arbitrators).
(7) Nothing in this section affects any right of the arbitrators, any expert, legal adviser or assessor appointed by the tribunal, or any arbitral institution, to payment of their fees and expenses.

Recoverable fees and expenses of arbitrators

64.—(1) Unless otherwise agreed by the parties, the recoverable costs of the arbitration shall include in respect of the fees and expenses of the arbitrators only such reasonable fees and expenses as are appropriate in the circumstances.
(2) If there is any question as to what reasonable fees and expenses are appropriate in the circumstances, and the matter is not already before the court on an application under section 63(4), the court may on the application of any party (upon notice to the other parties)—

(a) determine the matter, or

(b) order that it be determined by such means and upon such terms as the court may specify.

(3) Subsection (1) has effect subject to any order of the court under section 24(4) or 25(3)(b) (order as to entitlement to fees or expenses in case of removal or resignation of arbitrator).
(4) Nothing in this section affects any right of the arbitrator to payment of his fees and expenses.

Power to limit recoverable costs

65.—(1) Unless otherwise agreed by the parties, the tribunal may direct that the recoverable costs of the arbitration, or of any part of the arbitral proceedings, shall be limited to a specified amount.
(2) Any direction may be made or varied at any stage, but this must be done sufficiently in advance of the incurring of costs to which it relates, or the taking of any steps in the proceedings which may be affected by it, for the limit to be taken into account.

Powers of the court in relation to award

Enforcement of the award

66.—(1) An award made by the tribunal pursuant to an arbitration agreement may, by leave of the court, be enforced in the same manner as a judgment or order of the court to the same effect.
(2) Where leave is so given, judgment may be entered in terms of the award.
(3) Leave to enforce an award shall not be given where, or to the extent that, the person against whom it is sought to be enforced shows that the tribunal lacked substantive jurisdiction to make the award.
The right to raise such an objection may have been lost (see section 73).
(4) Nothing in this section affects the recognition or enforcement of an award under any other enactment or rule of law, in particular under Part II of the Arbitration Act 1950 (enforcement of awards under Geneva Convention) or the provisions of Part III of this Act relating to the recognition and enforcement of awards under the New York Convention or by an action on the award.

Challenging the award: substantive jurisdiction

67.—(1) A party to arbitral proceedings may (upon notice to the other parties and to the tribunal) apply to the court—

(a) challenging any award of the arbitral tribunal as to its substantive jurisdiction; or

(b) for an order declaring an award made by the tribunal on the merits to be of no effect, in whole or in part, because the tribunal did not have substantive jurisdiction.

A party may lose the right to object (see section 73) and the right to apply is subject to the restrictions in section 70(2) and (3).

(2) The arbitral tribunal may continue the arbitral proceedings and make a further award while an application to the court under this section is pending in relation to an award as to jurisdiction.
(3) On an application under this section challenging an award of the arbitral tribunal as to its substantive jurisdiction, the court may by order—

(a) confirm the award,

(b) vary the award, or

(c) set aside the award in whole or in part.

(4) The leave of the court is required for any appeal from a decision of the court under this section.

Challenging the award: serious irregularity

68.—(1) A party to arbitral proceedings may (upon notice to the other parties and to the tribunal) apply to the court challenging an award in the proceedings on the ground of serious irregularity affecting the tribunal, the proceedings or the award.
A party may lose the right to object (see section 73) and the right to apply is subject to the restrictions in section 70(2) and (3).
(2) Serious irregularity means an irregularity of one or more of the following kinds which the court considers has caused or will cause substantial injustice to the applicant—

(a) failure by the tribunal to comply with section 33 (general duty of tribunal);

(b) the tribunal exceeding its powers (otherwise than by exceeding its substantive jurisdiction: see section 67);

(c) failure by the tribunal to conduct the proceedings in accordance with the procedure agreed by the parties;

(d) failure by the tribunal to deal with all the issues that were put to it;

(e) any arbitral or other institution or person vested by the parties with powers in relation to the proceedings or the award exceeding its powers;

(f) uncertainty or ambiguity as to the effect of the award;

(g) the award being obtained by fraud or the award or the way in which it was procured being contrary to public policy;

(h) failure to comply with the requirements as to the form of the award; or

(i) any irregularity in the conduct of the proceedings or in the award which is admitted by the tribunal or by any arbitral or other institution or person vested by the parties with powers in relation to the proceedings or the award.

(3) If there is shown to be serious irregularity affecting the tribunal, the proceedings or the award, the court may—

(a) remit the award to the tribunal, in whole or in part, for reconsideration,

(b) set the award aside in whole or in part, or

(c) declare the award to be of no effect, in whole or in part.

The court shall not exercise its power to set aside or to declare an award to be of no effect, in whole or in part, unless it is satisfied that it would be inappropriate to remit the matters in question to the tribunal for reconsideration.

(4) The leave of the court is required for any appeal from a decision of the court under this section.

Appeal on point of law

69.—(1) Unless otherwise agreed by the parties, a party to arbitral proceedings may (upon notice to the other parties and to the tribunal) appeal to the court on a question of law arising out of an award made in the proceedings. An agreement to dispense with reasons for the tribunal's award shall be considered an agreement to exclude the court's jurisdiction under this section.

(2) An appeal shall not be brought under this section except—

(a) with the agreement of all the other parties to the proceedings, or

(b) with the leave of the court.

The right to appeal is also subject to the restrictions in section 70(2) and (3).

(3) Leave to appeal shall be given only if the court is satisfied—

(a) that the determination of the question will substantially affect the rights of one or more of the parties,

(b) that the question is one which the tribunal was asked to determine,

(c) that, on the basis of the findings of fact in the award—

(i) the decision of the tribunal on the question is obviously wrong, or

(ii) the question is one of general public importance and the decision of the tribunal is at least open to serious doubt, and

(d) that, despite the agreement of the parties to resolve the matter by arbitration, it is just and proper in all the circumstances for the court to determine the question.

(4) An application for leave to appeal under this section shall identify the question of law to be determined and state the grounds on which it is alleged that leave to appeal should be granted.

(5) The court shall determine an application for leave to appeal under this section without a hearing unless it appears to the court that a hearing is required.

(6) The leave of the court is required for any appeal from a decision of the court under this section to grant or refuse leave to appeal.
(7) On an appeal under this section the court may by order—

(a) confirm the award,

(b) vary the award,

(c) remit the award to the tribunal, in whole or in part, for reconsideration in the light of the court's determination, or

(d) set aside the award in whole or in part.

The court shall not exercise its power to set aside an award, in whole or in part, unless it is satisfied that it would be inappropriate to remit the matters in question to the tribunal for reconsideration.
(8) The decision of the court on an appeal under this section shall be treated as a judgment of the court for the purposes of a further appeal.
But no such appeal lies without the leave of the court which shall not be given unless the court considers that the question is one of general importance or is one which for some other special reason should be considered by the Court of Appeal.

Challenge or appeal: supplementary provisions

70.—(1) The following provisions apply to an application or appeal under section 67, 68 or 69.
(2) An application or appeal may not be brought if the applicant or appellant has not first exhausted—

(a) any available arbitral process of appeal or review, and

(b) any available recourse under section 57 (correction of award or additional award).

(3) Any application or appeal must be brought within 28 days of the date of the award or, if there has been any arbitral process of appeal or review, of the date when the applicant or appellant was notified of the result of that process.
(4) If on an application or appeal it appears to the court that the award—

(a) does not contain the tribunal's reasons, or

(b) does not set out the tribunal's reasons in sufficient detail to enable the court properly to consider the application or appeal,

the court may order the tribunal to state the reasons for its award in sufficient detail for that purpose.
(5) Where the court makes an order under subsection (4), it may make such further order as it thinks fit with respect to any additional costs of the arbitration resulting from its order.

(6) The court may order the applicant or appellant to provide security for the costs of the application or appeal, and may direct that the application or appeal be dismissed if the order is not complied with.
The power to order security for costs shall not be exercised on the ground that the applicant or appellant is—

(a) an individual ordinarily resident outside the United Kingdom, or

(b) a corporation or association incorporated or formed under the law of a country outside the United Kingdom, or whose central management and control is exercised outside the United Kingdom.

(7) The court may order that any money payable under the award shall be brought into court or otherwise secured pending the determination of the application or appeal, and may direct that the application or appeal be dismissed if the order is not complied with.
(8) The court may grant leave to appeal subject to conditions to the same or similar effect as an order under subsection (6) or (7).
This does not affect the general discretion of the court to grant leave subject to conditions.

Challenge or appeal: effect of order of court

71.—(1) The following provisions have effect where the court makes an order under section 67, 68 or 69 with respect to an award.
(2) Where the award is varied, the variation has effect as part of the tribunal's award.
(3) Where the award is remitted to the tribunal, in whole or in part, for reconsideration, the tribunal shall make a fresh award in respect of the matters remitted within three months of the date of the order for remission or such longer or shorter period as the court may direct.
(4) Where the award is set aside or declared to be of no effect, in whole or in part, the court may also order that any provision that an award is a condition precedent to the bringing of legal proceedings in respect of a matter to which the arbitration agreement applies, is of no effect as regards the subject matter of the award or, as the case may be, the relevant part of the award.

Miscellaneous

Saving for rights of person who takes no part in proceedings

72.—(1) A person alleged to be a party to arbitral proceedings but who takes no part in the proceedings may question—

(a) whether there is a valid arbitration agreement,

(b) whether the tribunal is properly constituted, or

(c) what matters have been submitted to arbitration in accordance with the arbitration agreement,

by proceedings in the court for a declaration or injunction or other appropriate relief.
(2) He also has the same right as a party to the arbitral proceedings to challenge an award—

(a) by an application under section 67 on the ground of lack of substantive jurisdiction in relation to him, or

(b) by an application under section 68 on the ground of serious irregularity (within the meaning of that section) affecting him;

and section 70(2) (duty to exhaust arbitral procedures) does not apply in his case.

Loss of right to object

73. —(1) If a party to arbitral proceedings takes part, or continues to take part, in the proceedings without making, either forthwith or within such time as is allowed by the arbitration agreement or the tribunal or by any provision of this Part, any objection—

(a) that the tribunal lacks substantive jurisdiction,

(b) that the proceedings have been improperly conducted,

(c) that there has been a failure to comply with the arbitration agreement or with any provision of this Part, or

(d) that there has been any other irregularity affecting the tribunal or the proceedings,

he may not raise that objection later, before the tribunal or the court, unless he shows that, at the time he took part or continued to take part in the proceedings, he did not know and could not with reasonable diligence have discovered the grounds for the objection.
(2) Where the arbitral tribunal rules that it has substantive jurisdiction and a party to arbitral proceedings who could have questioned that ruling—

(a) by any available arbitral process of appeal or review, or

(b) by challenging the award,

does not do so, or does not do so within the time allowed by the arbitration agreement or any provision of this Part, he may not object later to the tribunal's substantive jurisdiction on any ground which was the subject of that ruling.

Immunity of arbitral institutions, &c

74.—(1) An arbitral or other institution or person designated or requested by the parties to appoint or nominate an arbitrator is not liable for anything done or omitted in the discharge or purported discharge of

that function unless the act or omission is shown to have been in bad faith.
(2) An arbitral or other institution or person by whom an arbitrator is appointed or nominated is not liable, by reason of having appointed or nominated him, for anything done or omitted by the arbitrator (or his employees or agents) in the discharge or purported discharge of his functions as arbitrator.
(3) The above provisions apply to an employee or agent of an arbitral or other institution or person as they apply to the institution or person himself.

Charge to secure payment of solicitors' costs

75. —The powers of the court to make declarations and orders under section 73 of the Solicitors Act 1974 or Article 71H of the Solicitors (Northern Ireland) Order 1976 (power to charge property recovered in the proceedings with the payment of solicitors' costs) may be exercised in relation to arbitral proceedings as if those proceedings were proceedings in the court.

Supplementary

Service of notices, &c

76.—(1) The parties are free to agree on the manner of service of any notice or other document required or authorised to be given or served in pursuance of the arbitration agreement or for the purposes of the arbitral proceedings.
(2) If or to the extent that there is no such agreement the following provisions apply.
(3) A notice or other document may be served on a person by any effective means.
(4) If a notice or other document is addressed, pre-paid and delivered by post—

(a) to the addressee's last known principal residence or, if he is or has been carrying on a trade, profession or business, his last known principal business address, or

(b) where the addressee is a body corporate, to the body's registered or principal office,

it shall be treated as effectively served.
(5) This section does not apply to the service of documents for the purposes of legal proceedings, for which provision is made by rules of court.
(6) References in this Part to a notice or other document include any form of communication in writing and references to giving or serving a notice or other document shall be construed accordingly.

Powers of court in relation to service of documents

77.—(1) This section applies where service of a document on a person in the manner agreed by the parties, or in accordance with provisions of section 76 having effect in default of agreement, is not reasonably practicable.
(2) Unless otherwise agreed by the parties, the court may make such order as it thinks fit—

(a) for service in such manner as the court may direct, or

(b) dispensing with service of the document.

(3) Any party to the arbitration agreement may apply for an order, but only after exhausting any available arbitral process for resolving the matter.
(4) The leave of the court is required for any appeal from a decision of the court under this section.

Reckoning periods of time

78.—(1) The parties are free to agree on the method of reckoning periods of time for the purposes of any provision agreed by them or any provision of this Part having effect in default of such agreement.
(2) If or to the extent there is no such agreement, periods of time shall be reckoned in accordance with the following provisions.
(3) Where the act is required to be done within a specified period after or from a specified date, the period begins immediately after that date.
(4) Where the act is required to be done a specified number of clear days after a specified date, at least that number of days must intervene between the day on which the act is done and that date.
(5) Where the period is a period of seven days or less which would include a Saturday, Sunday or a public holiday in the place where anything which has to be done within the period falls to be done, that day shall be excluded. In relation to England and Wales or Northern Ireland, a "public holiday" means Christmas Day, Good Friday or a day which under the Banking and Financial Dealings Act 1971 is a bank holiday.

Power of court to extend time limits relating to arbitral proceedings

79.—(1) Unless the parties otherwise agree, the court may by order extend any time limit agreed by them in relation to any matter relating to the arbitral proceedings or specified in any provision of this Part having effect in default of such agreement.
This section does not apply to a time limit to which section 12 applies (power of court to extend time for beginning arbitral proceedings, &c.).
(2) An application for an order may be made—

(a) by any party to the arbitral proceedings (upon notice to the other parties and to the tribunal), or

(b) by the arbitral tribunal (upon notice to the parties).

(3) The court shall not exercise its power to extend a time limit unless it is satisfied—

(a) that any available recourse to the tribunal, or to any arbitral or other institution or person vested by the parties with power in that regard, has first been exhausted, and

(b) that a substantial injustice would otherwise be done.

(4) The court's power under this section may be exercised whether or not the time has already expired.
(5) An order under this section may be made on such terms as the court thinks fit.
(6) The leave of the court is required for any appeal from a decision of the court under this section.

Notice and other requirements in connection with legal proceedings

80.—(1) References in this Part to an application, appeal or other step in relation to legal proceedings being taken "upon notice" to the other parties to the arbitral proceedings, or to the tribunal, are to such notice of the originating process as is required by rules of court and do not impose any separate requirement.
(2) Rules of court shall be made—

(a) requiring such notice to be given as indicated by any provision of this Part, and

(b) as to the manner, form and content of any such notice.

(3) Subject to any provision made by rules of court, a requirement to give notice to the tribunal of legal proceedings shall be construed—

(a) if there is more than one arbitrator, as a requirement to give notice to each of them; and

(b) if the tribunal is not fully constituted, as a requirement to give notice to any arbitrator who has been appointed.

(4) References in this Part to making an application or appeal to the court within a specified period are to the issue within that period of the appropriate originating process in accordance with rules of court.
(5) Where any provision of this Part requires an application or appeal to be made to the court within a specified time, the rules of court relating to the reckoning of periods, the extending or abridging of periods, and the consequences of not taking a step within the period prescribed by the rules, apply in relation to that requirement.
(6) Provision may be made by rules of court amending the provisions of this Part—

(a) with respect to the time within which any application or appeal to the court must be made,

(b) so as to keep any provision made by this Part in relation to arbitral proceedings in step with the corresponding provision of rules of court applying in relation to proceedings in the court, or

(c) so as to keep any provision made by this Part in relation to legal proceedings in step with the corresponding provision of rules of court applying generally in relation to proceedings in the court.

(7) Nothing in this section affects the generality of the power to make rules of court.

Saving for certain matters governed by common law

81.—(1) Nothing in this Part shall be construed as excluding the operation of any rule of law consistent with the provisions of this Part, in particular, any rule of law as to—

(a) matters which are not capable of settlement by arbitration;

(b) the effect of an oral arbitration agreement; or

(c) the refusal of recognition or enforcement of an arbitral award on grounds of public policy.

(2) Nothing in this Act shall be construed as reviving any jurisdiction of the court to set aside or remit an award on the ground of errors of fact or law on the face of the award.

Minor definitions

82.—(1) In this Part—

"arbitrator", unless the context otherwise requires, includes an umpire;

"available arbitral process", in relation to any matter, includes any process of appeal to or review by an arbitral or other institution or person vested by the parties with powers in relation to that matter;

"claimant", unless the context otherwise requires, includes a counter-claimant, and related expressions shall be construed accordingly;

"dispute" includes any difference;

"enactment" includes an enactment contained in Northern Ireland legislation;

"legal proceedings" means civil proceedings in the High Court or a county court;

"peremptory order" means an order made under section 41(5) or made in exercise of any corresponding power conferred by the parties;

"premises" includes land, buildings, moveable structures, vehicles, vessels, aircraft and hovercraft;

"question of law" means—

(a) for a court in England and Wales, a question of the law of England and Wales, and

(b) for a court in Northern Ireland, a question of the law of Northern Ireland;

"substantive jurisdiction", in relation to an arbitral tribunal, refers to the matters specified in section 30(1)(a) to (c), and references to the tribunal exceeding its substantive jurisdiction shall be construed accordingly.

(2) References in this Part to a party to an arbitration agreement include any person claiming under or through a party to the agreement.

Index of defined expressions: Part I

83.—In this Part the expressions listed below are defined or otherwise explained by the provisions indicated—

agreement, agree and agreed	section 5(1)
agreement in writing	section 5(2) to (5)
arbitration agreement	sections 6 and 5(1)
arbitrator	section 82(1)
available arbitral process	section 82(1)
claimant	section 82(1)
commencement (in relation to arbitral proceedings)	section 14
costs of the arbitration	section 59
the court	section 105
dispute	section 82(1)
enactment	section 82(1)
legal proceedings	section 82(1)
Limitation Acts	section 13(4)
notice (or other document)	section 76(6)
party—	
– in relation to an arbitration agreement	section 82(2)
– where section 106(2) or (3) applies	section 106(4)
peremptory order	section 82(1) (and see section 41(5))
premises	section 82(1)
question of law	section 82(1)
recoverable costs	sections 63 and 64
seat of the arbitration	section 3
serve and service (of notice or other document)	section 76(6)
substantive jurisdiction (in relation to an arbitral tribunal)	section 82(1) (and see 30(1)(a) to (c))
upon notice (to the parties or the tribunal)	section 80
written and in writing	section 5(6)

Transitional provisions

84.—(1) The provisions of this Part do not apply to arbitral proceedings commenced before the date on which this Part comes into force.
(2) They apply to arbitral proceedings commenced on or after that date under an arbitration agreement whenever made.
(3) The above provisions have effect subject to any transitional provision made by an order under section 109(2) (power to include transitional provisions in commencement order).

PART II

OTHER PROVISIONS RELATING TO ARBITRATION

Domestic arbitration agreements

Modification of Part I in relation to domestic arbitration agreement

85.—(1) In the case of a domestic arbitration agreement the provisions of Part I are modified in accordance with the following sections.
(2) For this purpose a "domestic arbitration agreement" means an arbitration agreement to which none of the parties is—

(a) an individual who is a national of, or habitually resident in, a state other than the United Kingdom, or

(b) a body corporate which is incorporated in, or whose central control and management is exercised in, a state other than the United Kingdom,

and under which the seat of the arbitration (if the seat has been designated or determined) is in the United Kingdom.
(3) In subsection (2) "arbitration agreement" and "seat of the arbitration" have the same meaning as in Part I (see sections 3, 5(1) and 6).

Staying of legal proceedings

86.—(1) In section 9 (stay of legal proceedings), subsection (4) (stay unless the arbitration agreement is null and void, inoperative, or incapable of being performed) does not apply to a domestic arbitration agreement.
(2) On an application under that section in relation to a domestic arbitration agreement the court shall grant a stay unless satisfied—

(a) that the arbitration agreement is null and void, inoperative, or incapable of being performed, or

(b) that there are other sufficient grounds for not requiring the parties to abide by the arbitration agreement.

(3) The court may treat as a sufficient ground under subsection (2)(b) the fact that the applicant is or was at any material time not ready and willing

to do all things necessary for the proper conduct of the arbitration or of any other dispute resolution procedures required to be exhausted before resorting to arbitration.
(4) For the purposes of this section the question whether an arbitration agreement is a domestic arbitration agreement shall be determined by reference to the facts at the time the legal proceedings are commenced.

Effectiveness of agreement to exclude court's jurisdiction

87.—(1) In the case of a domestic arbitration agreement any agreement to exclude the jurisdiction of the court under—

(a) section 45 (determination of preliminary point of law), or

(b) section 69 (challenging the award: appeal on point of law),

is not effective unless entered into after the commencement of the arbitral proceedings in which the question arises or the award is made.
(2) For this purpose the commencement of the arbitral proceedings has the same meaning as in Part I (see section 14).
(3) For the purposes of this section the question whether an arbitration agreement is a domestic arbitration agreement shall be determined by reference to the facts at the time the agreement is entered into.

Power to repeal or amend sections 85 to 87

88.—(1) The Secretary of State may by order repeal or amend the provisions of sections 85 to 87.
(2) An order under this section may contain such supplementary, incidental and transitional provisions as appear to the Secretary of State to be appropriate.
(3) An order under this section shall be made by statutory instrument and no such order shall be made unless a draft of it has been laid before and approved by a resolution of each House of Parliament.

Consumer arbitration agreements

Application of unfair terms regulations to consumer arbitration agreements

89.—(1) The following sections extend the application of the Unfair Terms in Consumer Contracts Regulations 1994 in relation to a term which constitutes an arbitration agreement.

For this purpose "arbitration agreement" means an agreement to submit to arbitration present or future disputes or differences (whether or not contractual).
(2) In those sections "the Regulations" means those regulations and includes any regulations amending or replacing those regulations.
(3) Those sections apply whatever the law applicable to the arbitration agreement.

Regulations apply where consumer is a legal person

90.—The Regulations apply where the consumer is a legal person as they apply where the consumer is a natural person.

Arbitration agreement unfair where modest amount sought

91.—(1) A term which constitutes an arbitration agreement is unfair for the purposes of the Regulations so far as it relates to a claim for a pecuniary remedy which does not exceed the amount specified by order for the purposes of this section.
(2) Orders under this section may make different provision for different cases and for different purposes.
(3) The power to make orders under this section is exercisable—

(a) for England and Wales, by the Secretary of State with the concurrence of the Lord Chancellor,

(b) for Scotland, by the Secretary of State with the concurrence of the Lord Advocate, and

(c) for Northern Ireland, by the Department of Economic Development for Northern Ireland with the concurrence of the Lord Chancellor.

(4) Any such order for England and Wales or Scotland shall be made by statutory instrument which shall be subject to annulment in pursuance of a resolution of either House of Parliament.
(5) Any such order for Northern Ireland shall be a statutory rule for the purposes of the Statutory Rules (Northern Ireland) Order 1979 and shall be subject to negative resolution, within the meaning of section 41(6) of the Interpretation Act (Northern Ireland) 1954.

Small claims arbitration in the county court

Exclusion of Part I in relation to small claims arbitration in the county court

92.—Nothing in Part I of this Act applies to arbitration under section 64 of the County Courts Act 1984.

Appointment of judges as arbitrators

Appointment of judges as arbitrators

93.—(1) A judge of the Commercial Court or an official referee may, if in all the circumstances he thinks fit, accept appointment as a sole arbitrator or as umpire by or by virtue of an arbitration agreement.
(2) A judge of the Commercial Court shall not do so unless the Lord Chief Justice has informed him that, having regard to the state of business in the High Court and the Crown Court, he can be made available.

(3) An official referee shall not do so unless the Lord Chief Justice has informed him that, having regard to the state of official referees' business, he can be made available.
(4) The fees payable for the services of a judge of the Commercial Court or official referee as arbitrator or umpire shall be taken in the High Court.
(5) In this section—
"arbitration agreement" has the same meaning as in Part I; and
"official referee" means a person nominated under section 68(1)(a) of the Supreme Court Act 1981 to deal with official referees' business.
(6) The provisions of Part I of this Act apply to arbitration before a person appointed under this section with the modifications specified in Schedule 2.

Statutory arbitrations

Application of Part I to statutory arbitrations

94.—(1) The provisions of Part I apply to every arbitration under an enactment (a "statutory arbitration"), whether the enactment was passed or made before or after the commencement of this Act, subject to the adaptations and exclusions specified in sections 95 to 98.
(2) The provisions of Part I do not apply to a statutory arbitration if or to the extent that their application—

(a) is inconsistent with the provisions of the enactment concerned, with any rules or procedure authorised or recognised by it, or

(b) is excluded by any other enactment.

(3) In this section and the following provisions of this Part "enactment"—

(a) in England and Wales, includes an enactment contained in subordinate legislation within the meaning of the Interpretation Act 1978;

(b) in Northern Ireland, means a statutory provision within the meaning of section 1(f) of the Interpretation Act (Northern Ireland) 1954.

General adaptation of provisions in relation to statutory arbitrations

95.—(1) The provisions of Part I apply to a statutory arbitration—

(a) as if the arbitration were pursuant to an arbitration agreement and as if the enactment were that agreement, and

(b) as if the persons by and against whom a claim subject to arbitration in pursuance of the enactment may be or has been made were parties to that agreement.

(2) Every statutory arbitration shall be taken to have its seat in England and Wales or, as the case may be, in Northern Ireland.

Specific adaptations of provisions in relation to statutory arbitrations

96.—(1) The following provisions of Part I apply to a statutory arbitration with the following adaptations.
(2) In section 30(1) (competence of tribunal to rule on its own jurisdiction), the reference in paragraph (a) to whether there is a valid arbitration agreement shall be construed as a reference to whether the enactment applies to the dispute or difference in question.
(3) Section 35 (consolidation of proceedings and concurrent hearings) applies only so as to authorise the consolidation of proceedings, or concurrent hearings in proceedings, under the same enactment.
(4) Section 46 (rules applicable to substance of dispute) applies with the omission of subsection (1)(b) (determination in accordance with considerations agreed by parties).

Provisions excluded from applying to statutory arbitrations

97.—The following provisions of Part I do not apply in relation to a statutory arbitration—

(a) section 8 (whether agreement discharged by death of a party);
(b) section 12 (power of court to extend agreed time limits);
(c) sections 9(5), 10(2) and 71(4) (restrictions on effect of provision that award condition precedent to right to bring legal proceedings).

Power to make further provision by regulations

98.—(1) The Secretary of State may make provision by regulations for adapting or excluding any provision of Part I in relation to statutory arbitrations in general or statutory arbitrations of any particular description.
(2) The power is exercisable whether the enactment concerned is passed or made before or after the commencement of this Act.
(3) Regulations under this section shall be made by statutory instrument which shall be subject to annulment in pursuance of a resolution of either House of Parliament.

Part III

Recognition and enforcement of Certain Foreign Awards

Enforcement of Geneva Convention awards

Continuation of Part II of the Arbitration Act 1950

99.—Part II of the Arbitration Act 1950 (enforcement of certain foreign awards) continues to apply in relation to foreign awards within the meaning of that Part which are not also New York Convention awards.

New York Convention awards

100.—(1) In this Part a "New York Convention award" means an award made, in pursuance of an arbitration agreement, in the territory of a state (other than the United Kingdom) which is a party to the New York Convention.

(2) For the purposes of subsection (1) and of the provisions of this Part relating to such awards—

(a) "arbitration agreement" means an arbitration agreement in writing, and

(b) an award shall be treated as made at the seat of the arbitration, regardless of where it was signed, despatched or delivered to any of the parties.

In this subsection "agreement in writing" and "seat of the arbitration" have the same meaning as in Part I.

(3) If Her Majesty by Order in Council declares that a state specified in the Order is a party to the New York Convention, or is a party in respect of any territory so specified, the Order shall, while in force, be conclusive evidence of that fact.

(4) In this section "the New York Convention" means the Convention on the Recognition and Enforcement of Foreign Arbitral Awards adopted by the United Nations Conference on International Commercial Arbitration on 10th June 1958.

Recognition and enforcement of awards

101.—(1) A New York Convention award shall be recognised as binding on the persons as between whom it was made, and may accordingly be relied on by those persons by way of defence, set-off or otherwise in any legal proceedings in England and Wales or Northern Ireland.

(2) A New York Convention award may, by leave of the court, be enforced in the same manner as a judgment or order of the court to the same effect.

As to the meaning of "the court" see section 105.

(3) Where leave is so given, judgment may be entered in terms of the award.

Evidence to be produced by party seeking recognition or enforcement

102.—(1) A party seeking the recognition or enforcement of a New York Convention award must produce—

(a) the duly authenticated original award or a duly certified copy of it, and

(b) the original arbitration agreement or a duly certified copy of it.

(2) If the award or agreement is in a foreign language, the party must also produce a translation of it certified by an official or sworn translator or by a diplomatic or consular agent.

Refusal of recognition or enforcement

103.—(1) Recognition or enforcement of a New York Convention award shall not be refused except in the following cases.
(2) Recognition or enforcement of the award may be refused if the person against whom it is invoked proves—

(a) that a party to the arbitration agreement was (under the law applicable to him) under some incapacity;

(b) that the arbitration agreement was not valid under the law to which the parties subjected it or, failing any indication thereon, under the law of the country where the award was made;

(c) that he was not given proper notice of the appointment of the arbitrator or of the arbitration proceedings or was otherwise unable to present his case;

(d) that the award deals with a difference not contemplated by or not falling within the terms of the submission to arbitration or contains decisions on matters beyond the scope of the submission to arbitration (but see subsection (4));

(e) that the composition of the arbitral tribunal or the arbitral procedure was not in accordance with the agreement of the parties or, failing such agreement, with the law of the country in which the arbitration took place;

(f) that the award has not yet become binding on the parties, or has been set aside or suspended by a competent authority of the country in which, or under the law of which, it was made.

(3) Recognition or enforcement of the award may also be refused if the award is in respect of a matter which is not capable of settlement by arbitration, or if it would be contrary to public policy to recognise or enforce the award.
(4) An award which contains decisions on matters not submitted to arbitration may be recognised or enforced to the extent that it contains decisions on matters submitted to arbitration which can be separated from those on matters not so submitted.
(5) Where an application for the setting aside or suspension of the award has been made to such a competent authority as is mentioned in subsection (2)(f), the court before which the award is sought to be relied upon may, if it considers it proper, adjourn the decision on the recognition or enforcement of the award.
It may also on the application of the party claiming recognition or enforcement of the award order the other party to give suitable security.

Saving for other bases of recognition or enforcement

104.—Nothing in the preceding provisions of this Part affects any right to rely upon or enforce a New York Convention award at common law or under section 66.

Part IV

General Provisions

Meaning of "the court": jurisdiction of High Court and county court

105.—(1) In this Act "the court" means the High Court or a county court, subject to the following provisions.
(2) The Lord Chancellor may by order make provision—

(a) allocating proceedings under this Act to the High Court or to county courts; or

(b) specifying proceedings under this Act which may be commenced or taken only in the High Court or in a county court.

(3) The Lord Chancellor may by order make provision requiring proceedings of any specified description under this Act in relation to which a county court has jurisdiction to be commenced or taken in one or more specified county courts.
Any jurisdiction so exercisable by a specified county court is exercisable throughout England and Wales or, as the case may be, Northern Ireland.
(4) An order under this section—

(a) may differentiate between categories of proceedings by reference to such criteria as the Lord Chancellor sees fit to specify, and

(b) may make such incidental or transitional provision as the Lord Chancellor considers necessary or expedient.

(5) An order under this section for England and Wales shall be made by statutory instrument which shall be subject to annulment in pursuance of a resolution of either House of Parliament.
(6) An order under this section for Northern Ireland shall be a statutory rule for the purposes of the Statutory Rules (Northern Ireland) Order 1979 which shall be subject to annulment in pursuance of a resolution of either House of Parliament in like manner as a statutory instrument and section 5 of the Statutory Instruments Act 1946 shall apply accordingly.

Crown application

106.—(1) Part I of this Act applies to any arbitration agreement to which Her Majesty, either in right of the Crown or of the Duchy of Lancaster or otherwise, or the Duke of Cornwall, is a party.

(2) Where Her Majesty is party to an arbitration agreement otherwise than in right of the Crown, Her Majesty shall be represented for the purposes of any arbitral proceedings—

(a) where the agreement was entered into by Her Majesty in right of the Duchy of Lancaster, by the Chancellor of the Duchy or such person as he may appoint, and

(b) in any other case, by such person as Her Majesty may appoint in writing under the Royal Sign Manual.

(3) Where the Duke of Cornwall is party to an arbitration agreement, he shall be represented for the purposes of any arbitral proceedings by such person as he may appoint.

(4) References in Part I to a party or the parties to the arbitration agreement or to arbitral proceedings shall be construed, where subsection (2) or (3) applies, as references to the person representing Her Majesty or the Duke of Cornwall.

Consequential amendments and repeals

107.—(1) The enactments specified in Schedule 3 are amended in accordance with that Schedule, the amendments being consequential on the provisions of this Act.

(2) The enactments specified in Schedule 4 are repealed to the extent specified.

Extent

108.—(1) The provisions of this Act extend to England and Wales and, except as mentioned below, to Northern Ireland.

(2) The following provisions of Part II do not extend to Northern Ireland—

section 92 (exclusion of Part I in relation to small claims arbitration in the county court), and

section 93 and Schedule 2 (appointment of judges as arbitrators).

(3) Sections 89, 90 and 91 (consumer arbitration agreements) extend to Scotland and the provisions of Schedules 3 and 4 (consequential amendments and repeals) extend to Scotland so far as they relate to enactments which so extend, subject as follows.

(4) The repeal of the Arbitration Act 1975 extends only to England and Wales and Northern Ireland.

Commencement

109.—(1) The provisions of this Act come into force on such day as the Secretary of State may appoint by order made by statutory instrument, and different days may be appointed for different purposes.

(2) An order under subsection (1) may contain such transitional provisions as appear to the Secretary of State to be appropriate.

Short title

110.—This Act may be cited as the Arbitration Act 1996.

SCHEDULES

SCHEDULE 1

Section 4(1)

Mandatory Provisions or Part I

sections 9 to 11 (stay of legal proceedings);
section 12 (power of court to extend agreed time limits);
section 13 (application of Limitation Acts);
section 24 (power of court to remove arbitrator);
section 26(1) (effect of death of arbitrator);
section 28 (liability of parties for fees and expenses of arbitrators);
section 29 (immunity of arbitrator);
section 31 (objection to substantive jurisdiction of tribunal);
section 32 (determination of preliminary point of jurisdiction);
section 33 (general duty of tribunal);
section 37(2) (items to be treated as expenses of arbitrators);
section 40 (general duty of parties);
section 43 (securing the attendance of witnesses);
section 56 (power to withhold award in case of non-payment);
section 60 (effectiveness of agreement for payment of costs in any event);
section 66 (enforcement of award);
sections 67 and 68 (challenging the award: substantive jurisdiction and serious irregularity), and sections 70 and 71 (supplementary provisions; effect of order of court) so far as relating to those sections;
section 72 (saving for rights of person who takes no part in proceedings);
section 73 (loss of right to object);
section 74 (immunity of arbitral institutions, &c.);
section 75 (charge to secure payment of solicitors' costs).

SCHEDULE 2

Section 93(6)

Modifications of Part I in Relation to Judge-Arbitrators

Introductory

1.—In this Schedule "judge-arbitrator" means a judge of the Commercial Court or official referee appointed as arbitrator or umpire under section 93.

General

2.—(1) Subject to the following provisions of this Schedule, references in Part I to the court shall be construed in relation to a judge-arbitrator, or in relation to the appointment of a judge-arbitrator, as references to the Court of Appeal.
(2) The references in sections 32(6), 45(6) and 69(8) to the Court of Appeal shall in such a case be construed as references to the House of Lords.

Arbitrator's fees

3.—(1) The power of the court in section 28(2) to order consideration and adjustment of the liability of a party for the fees of an arbitrator may be exercised by a judge-arbitrator.
(2) Any such exercise of the power is subject to the powers of the Court of Appeal under sections 24(4) and 25(3)(b) (directions as to entitlement to fees or expenses in case of removal or resignation).

Exercise of court powers in support of arbitration

4.—(1) Where the arbitral tribunal consists of or includes a judge-arbitrator the powers of the court under sections 42 to 44 (enforcement of peremptory orders, summoning witnesses, and other court powers) are exercisable by the High Court and also by the judge-arbitrator himself.
(2) Anything done by a judge-arbitrator in the exercise of those powers shall be regarded as done by him in his capacity as judge of the High Court and have effect as if done by that court.
Nothing in this sub-paragraph prejudices any power vested in him as arbitrator or umpire.

Extension of time for making award

5.—(1) The power conferred by section 50 (extension of time for making award) is exercisable by the judge-arbitrator himself.
(2) Any appeal from a decision of a judge-arbitrator under that section lies to the Court of Appeal with the leave of that court.

Withholding award in case of non-payment

6.—(1) The provisions of paragraph 7 apply in place of the provisions of section 56 (power to withhold award in the case of non-payment) in relation to the withholding of an award for non-payment of the fees and expenses of a judge-arbitrator.
(2) This does not affect the application of section 56 in relation to the delivery of such an award by an arbitral or other institution or person vested by the parties with powers in relation to the delivery of the award.

7.—(1) A judge-arbitrator may refuse to deliver an award except upon payment of the fees and expenses mentioned in section 56(1).
(2) The judge-arbitrator may, on an application by a party to the arbitral proceedings, order that if he pays into the High Court the fees and expenses demanded, or such lesser amount as the judge-arbitrator may specify—

(a) the award shall be delivered,

(b) the amount of the fees and expenses properly payable shall be determined by such means and upon such terms as he may direct, and

(c) out of the money paid into court there shall be paid out such fees and expenses as may be found to be properly payable and the balance of the money (if any) shall be paid out to the applicant.

(3) For this purpose the amount of fees and expenses properly payable is the amount the applicant is liable to pay under section 28 or any agreement relating to the payment of the arbitrator.
(4) No application to the judge-arbitrator under this paragraph may be made where there is any available arbitral process for appeal or review of the amount of the fees or expenses demanded.
(5) Any appeal from a decision of a judge-arbitrator under this paragraph lies to the Court of Appeal with the leave of that court.
(6) Where a party to arbitral proceedings appeals under sub-paragraph (5), an arbitrator is entitled to appear and be heard.

Correction of award or additional award

8.—Subsections (4) to (6) of section 57 (correction of award or additional award: time limit for application or exercise of power) do not apply to a judge-arbitrator.

Costs

9.—Where the arbitral tribunal consists of or includes a judge-arbitrator the powers of the court under section 63(4) (determination of recoverable costs) shall be exercised by the High Court.
10. —(1) The power of the court under section 64 to determine an arbitrator's reasonable fees and expenses may be exercised by a judge-arbitrator.
(2) Any such exercise of the power is subject to the powers of the Court of Appeal under sections 24(4) and 25(3)(b) (directions as to entitlement to fees or expenses in case of removal or resignation).

Enforcement of award

11.—The leave of the court required by section 66 (enforcement of award) may in the case of an award of a judge-arbitrator be given by the judge-arbitrator himself.

Solicitors' costs

12.—The powers of the court to make declarations and orders under the provisions applied by section 75 (power to charge property recovered in arbitral proceedings with the payment of solicitors' costs) may be exercised by the judge-arbitrator.

Powers of court in relation to service of documents

13.—(1) The power of the court under section 77(2) (powers of court in relation to service of documents) is exercisable by the judge-arbitrator.
(2) Any appeal from a decision of a judge-arbitrator under that section lies to the Court of Appeal with the leave of that court.

Powers of court to extend time limits relating to arbitral proceedings

14.—(1) The power conferred by section 79 (power of court to extend time limits relating to arbitral proceedings) is exercisable by the judge-arbitrator himself.
(2) Any appeal from a decision of a judge-arbitrator under that section lies to the Court of Appeal with the leave of that court.

SCHEDULE 3

Section 107(1)

Consequential Amendments

Merchant Shipping Act 1894 (c.60)

1.—In section 496 of the Merchant Shipping Act 1894 (provisions as to deposits by owners of goods), after subsection (4) insert—

"(5) In subsection (3) the expression "legal proceedings" includes arbitral proceedings and as respects England and Wales and Northern Ireland the provisions of section 14 of the Arbitration Act 1996 apply to determine when such proceedings are commenced.".

Stannaries Court (Abolition) Act 1896 (c.45)

2—In section 4(1) of the Stannaries Court (Abolition) Act 1896 (references of certain disputes to arbitration), for the words from "tried before" to "any such reference" substitute "referred to arbitration before himself or before an arbitrator agreed on by the parties or an officer of the court".

Tithe Act 1936 (c.43)

3.—In section 39(1) of the Tithe Act 1936 (proceedings of Tithe Redemption Commission)—

(a) for "the Arbitration Acts 1889 to 1934" substitute "Part I of the Arbitration Act 1996";

(b) for paragraph (e) substitute—"(e) the making of an application to the court to determine a preliminary point of law and the bringing of an appeal to the court on a point of law;";

(c) for "the said Acts" substitute "Part I of the Arbitration Act 1996".

Education Act 1944 (c.31)

4.—In section 75(2) of the Education Act 1944 (proceedings of Independent School Tribunals) for "the Arbitration Acts 1889 to 1934" substitute "Part I of the Arbitration Act 1996".

Commonwealth Telegraphs Act 1949 (c.39)

5.—In section 8(2) of the Commonwealth Telegraphs Act 1949 (proceedings of referees under the Act) for "the Arbitration Acts 1889 to 1934, or the Arbitration Act (Northern Ireland) 1937," substitute "Part I of the Arbitration Act 1996".

Lands Tribunal Act 1949 (c.42)

6.—In section 3 of the Lands Tribunal Act 1949 (proceedings before the Lands Tribunal)—

(a) in subsection (6)(c) (procedural rules: power to apply Arbitration Acts), and

(b) in subsection (8) (exclusion of Arbitration Acts except as applied by rules),

for "the Arbitration Acts 1889 to 1934" substitute "Part I of the Arbitration Act 1996".

Wireless Telegraphy Act 1949 (c.54)

7.—In the Wireless Telegraphy Act 1949, Schedule 2 (procedure of appeals tribunal), in paragraph 3(1)—

(a) for the words "the Arbitration Acts 1889 to 1934" substitute "Part I of the Arbitration Act 1996";

(b) after the word "Wales" insert "or Northern Ireland"; and

(c) for "the said Acts" substitute "Part I of that Act".

Patents Act 1949 (c.87)

8.—In section 67 of the Patents Act 1949 (proceedings as to infringement of pre-1978 patents referred to comptroller), for "The Arbitration Acts 1889 to 1934" substitute "Part I of the Arbitration Act 1996".

National Health Service (Amendment) Act 1949 (c.93)

9.—In section 7(8) of the National Health Service (Amendment) Act 1949 (arbitration in relation to hardship arising from the National Health Service Act 1946 or the Act), for "the Arbitration Acts 1889 to 1934" substitute "Part I of the Arbitration Act 1996" and for "the said Acts" substitute "Part I of that Act".

Arbitration Act 1950 (c.27)

10.—In section 36(1) of the Arbitration Act 1950 (effect of foreign awards enforceable under Part II of that Act) for "section 26 of this Act" substitute "section 66 of the Arbitration Act 1996".

Interpretation Act (Northern Ireland) 1954 (c.33 (N.I.))

11.—In section 46(2) of the Interpretation Act (Northern Ireland) 1954 (miscellaneous definitions), for the definition of "arbitrator" substitute—

"'arbitrator' has the same meaning as in Part I of the Arbitration Act 1996;".

Agricultural Marketing Act 1958 (c.47)

12.—In section 12(1) of the Agricultural Marketing Act 1958 (application of provisions of Arbitration Act 1950)—

(a) for the words from the beginning to "shall apply" substitute "Sections 45 and 69 of the Arbitration Act 1996 (which relate to the determination by the court of questions of law) and section 66 of that Act (enforcement of awards) apply"; and

(b) for "an arbitration" substitute "arbitral proceedings".

Carriage by Air Act 1961 (c.27)

13.—(1) The Carriage by Air Act 1961 is amended as follows.
(2) In section 5(3) (time for bringing proceedings)—

(a) for "an arbitration" in the first place where it occurs substitute "arbitral proceedings"; and

(b) for the words from "and subsections (3) and (4)" to the end substitute "and the provisions of section 14 of the Arbitration Act 1996 apply to determine when such proceedings are commenced.".

(3) In section 11(c) (application of section 5 to Scotland)—

(a) for "subsections (3) and (4)" substitute "the provisions of section 14 of the Arbitration Act 1996"; and

(b) for "an arbitration" substitute "arbitral proceedings".

Factories Act 1961 (c.34)

14.—In the Factories Act 1961, for section 171 (application of Arbitration Act 1950), substitute—

171. "Application of the Arbitration Act 1996. Part I of the Arbitration Act 1996 does not apply to proceedings under this Act except in so far as it may be applied by regulations made under this Act.".

Clergy Pensions Measure 1961 (No. 3)

15.—In the Clergy Pensions Measure 1961, section 38(4) (determination of questions), for the words "The Arbitration Act 1950" substitute "Part I of the Arbitration Act 1996".

Transport Act 1962 (c.46)

16.—(1) The Transport Act 1962 is amended as follows.
(2) In section 74(6)(f) (proceedings before referees in pension disputes), for the words "the Arbitration Act 1950" substitute "Part I of the Arbitration Act 1996".
(3) In section 81(7) (proceedings before referees in compensation disputes), for the words "the Arbitration Act 1950" substitute "Part I of the Arbitration Act 1996".
(4) In Schedule 7, Part IV (pensions), in paragraph 17(5) for the words "the Arbitration Act 1950" substitute "Part I of the Arbitration Act 1996".

Corn Rents Act 1963 (c.14)

17.—In the Corn Rents Act 1963, section 1(5) (schemes for apportioning corn rents, &c.), for the words "the Arbitration Act 1950" substitute "Part I of the Arbitration Act 1996".

Plant Varieties and Seeds Act 1964 (c.14)

18.—In section 10(6) of the Plant Varieties and Seeds Act 1964 (meaning of "arbitration agreement"), for "the meaning given by section 32 of the

Arbitration Act 1950" substitute "the same meaning as in Part I of the Arbitration Act 1996".

Lands Tribunal and Compensation Act (Northern Ireland) 1964 (c.29 (N.I.))

19.—In section 9 of the Lands Tribunal and Compensation Act (Northern Ireland) 1964 (proceedings of Lands Tribunal), in subsection (3) (where Tribunal acts as arbitrator) for "the Arbitration Act (Northern Ireland) 1937" substitute "Part I of the Arbitration Act 1996".

Industrial and Provident Societies Act 1965 (c.12)

20.—(1) Section 60 of the Industrial and Provident Societies Act 1965 is amended as follows.

(2) In subsection (8) (procedure for hearing disputes between society and member, &c.)—

(a) in paragraph (a) for "the Arbitration Act 1950" substitute "Part I of the Arbitration Act 1996"; and

(b) in paragraph (b) omit "by virtue of section 12 of the said Act of 1950".

(3) For subsection (9) substitute—

"(9) The court or registrar to whom any dispute is referred under subsections (2) to (7) may at the request of either party state a case on any question of law arising in the dispute for the opinion of the High Court or, as the case may be, the Court of Session.".

Carriage of Goods by Road Act 1965 (c.37)

21.—In section 7(2) of the Carriage of Goods by Road Act 1965 (arbitrations: time at which deemed to commence), for paragraphs (a) and (b) substitute—

"(a) as respects England and Wales and Northern Ireland, the provisions of section 14(3) to (5) of the Arbitration Act 1996 (which determine the time at which an arbitration is commenced) apply;".

Factories Act (Northern Ireland) 1965 (c.20 (N.I.))

22.—In section 171 of the Factories Act (Northern Ireland) 1965 (application of Arbitration Act), for "The Arbitration Act (Northern Ireland) 1937" substitute "Part I of the Arbitration Act 1996".

Commonwealth Secretariat Act 1966 (c.10)

23.—In section 1(3) of the Commonwealth Secretariat Act 1966 (contracts with Commonwealth Secretariat to be deemed to contain provision for arbitration), for "the Arbitration Act 1950 and the Arbitration Act (Northern Ireland) 1937" substitute "Part I of the Arbitration Act 1996".

Arbitration (International Investment Disputes) Act 1966 (c.41)

24.—In the Arbitration (International Investment Disputes) Act 1966, for section 3 (application of Arbitration Act 1950 and other enactments) substitute—

"Application of provisions of Arbitration Act 1996

3.—(1) The Lord Chancellor may by order direct that any of the provisions contained in sections 36 and 38 to 44 of the Arbitration Act 1996 (provisions concerning the conduct of arbitral proceedings, &c.) shall apply to such proceedings pursuant to the Convention as are specified in the order with or without any modifications or exceptions specified in the order.

(2) Subject to subsection (1), the Arbitration Act 1996 shall not apply to proceedings pursuant to the Convention, but this subsection shall not be taken as affecting section 9 of that Act (stay of legal proceedings in respect of matter subject to arbitration).

(3) An order made under this section—

(a) may be varied or revoked by a subsequent order so made, and

(b) shall be contained in a statutory instrument."

Poultry Improvement Act (Northern Ireland) 1968 (c.12 (N.I.))

25.—In paragraph 10(4) of the Schedule to the Poultry Improvement Act (Northern Ireland) 1968 (reference of disputes), for "The Arbitration Act (Northern Ireland) 1937" substitute "Part I of the Arbitration Act 1996".

Industrial and Provident Societies Act (Northern Ireland) 1969 (c.24 (N.I.))

26.—(1) Section 69 of the Industrial and Provident Societies Act (Northern Ireland) 1969 (decision of disputes) is amended as follows.

(2) In subsection (7) (decision of disputes)—

(a) in the opening words, omit the words from "and without prejudice" to "1937";

(b) at the beginning of paragraph (a) insert "without prejudice to any powers exercisable by virtue of Part I of the Arbitration Act 1996,"; and

(c) in paragraph (b) omit "the registrar or" and "registrar or" and for the words from "as might have been granted by the High Court" to the end substitute "as might be granted by the registrar".

(3) For subsection (8) substitute—

"(8) The court or registrar to whom any dispute is referred under subsections (2) to (6) may at the request of either party state a case on any question of law arising in the dispute for the opinion of the High Court."

Health and Personal Social Services (Northern Ireland) Order 1972 (N.I.14)

27. —In Article 105(6) of the Health and Personal Social Services (Northern Ireland) Order 1972 (arbitrations under the Order), for "the Arbitration Act (Northern Ireland) 1937" substitute "Part I of the Arbitration Act 1996".

Consumer Credit Act 1974 (c.39)

28.—(1) Section 146 of the Consumer Credit Act 1974 is amended as follows.

(2) In subsection (2) (solicitor engaged in contentious business), for "section 86(1) of the Solicitors Act 1957" substitute "section 87(1) of the Solicitors Act 1974".

(3) In subsection (4) (solicitor in Northern Ireland engaged in contentious business), for the words from "business done" to "Administration of Estates (Northern Ireland) Order 1979" substitute "contentious business (as defined in Article 3(2) of the Solicitors (Northern Ireland) Order 1976."

Friendly Societies Act 1974 (c.46)

29.—(1) The Friendly Societies Act 1974 is amended as follows.

(2) For section 78(1) (statement of case) substitute—

"(1) Any arbitrator, arbiter or umpire to whom a dispute falling within section 76 above is referred under the rules of a registered society or branch may at the request of either party state a case on any question of law arising in the dispute for the opinion of the High Court or, as the case may be, the Court of Session."

(3) In section 83(3) (procedure on objections to amalgamations &c. of friendly societies), for "the Arbitration Act 1950 or, in Northern Ireland, the Arbitration Act (Northern Ireland) 1937" substitute "Part I of the Arbitration Act 1996".

Industry Act 1975 (c.68)

30.—In Schedule 3 to the Industry Act (arbitration of disputes relating to vesting and compensation orders), in paragraph 14 (application of certain provisions of Arbitration Acts)—

(a) for "the Arbitration Act 1950 or, in Northern Ireland, the Arbitration Act (Northern Ireland) 1937" substitute "Part I of the Arbitration Act 1996", and

(b) for "that Act" substitute "that Part".

Industrial Relations (Northern Ireland) Order 1976 (N.I.16)

31.—In Article 59(9) of the Industrial Relations (Northern Ireland) Order 1976 (proceedings of industrial tribunal), for "The Arbitration Act (Northern Ireland) 1937" substitute "Part I of the Arbitration Act 1996".

Aircraft and Shipbuilding Industries Act 1977 (c.3)

32.—In Schedule 7 to the Aircraft and Shipbuilding Industries Act 1977 (procedure of Arbitration Tribunal), in paragraph 2–

(a) for "the Arbitration Act 1950 or, in Northern Ireland, the Arbitration Act (Northern Ireland) 1937" substitute "Part I of the Arbitration Act 1996", and

(b) for "that Act" substitute "that Part".

Patents Act 1977 (c.37)

33.—In section 130 of the Patents Act 1977 (interpretation), in subsection (8) (exclusion of Arbitration Act) for "The Arbitration Act 1950" substitute "Part I of the Arbitration Act 1996".

Judicature (Northern Ireland) Act 1978 (c.23)

34.—(1) The Judicature (Northern Ireland) Act 1978 is amended as follows.
(2) In section 35(2) (restrictions on appeals to the Court of Appeal), after paragraph (f) insert—

"(fa) except as provided by Part I of the Arbitration Act 1996, from any decision of the High Court under that Part;".

(3) In section 55(2) (rules of court) after paragraph (c) insert—

"(cc) providing for any prescribed part of the jurisdiction of the High Court in relation to the trial of any action involving matters of account to be exercised in the prescribed manner by a person agreed by the parties and for the remuneration of any such person;".

Health and Safety at Work (Northern Ireland) Order 1978 (N.I.9)

35.—In Schedule 4 to the Health and Safety at Work (Northern Ireland) Order 1978 (licensing provisions), in paragraph 3, for "The Arbitration Act (Northern Ireland) 1937" substitute "Part I of the Arbitration Act 1996".

County Courts (Northern Ireland) Order 1980 (N.I.3)

36.—(1) The County Courts (Northern Ireland) Order 1980 is amended as follows.

(2) In Article 30 (civil jurisdiction exercisable by district judge)—

(a) for paragraph (2) substitute—

"(2) Any order, decision or determination made by a district judge under this Article (other than one made in dealing with a claim by way of arbitration under paragraph (3)) shall be embodied in a decree which for all purposes (including the right of appeal under Part VI) shall have the like effect as a decree pronounced by a county court judge.";

(b) for paragraphs (4) and (5) substitute—

"(4) Where in any action to which paragraph (1) applies the claim is dealt with by way of arbitration under paragraph (3)—

(a) any award made by the district judge in dealing with the claim shall be embodied in a decree which for all purposes (except the right of appeal under Part VI) shall have the like effect as a decree pronounced by a county court judge;

(b) the district judge may, and shall if so required by the High Court, state for the determination of the High Court any question of law arising out of an award so made;

(c) except as provided by sub-paragraph (b), any award so made shall be final; and

(d) except as otherwise provided by county court rules, no costs shall be awarded in connection with the action.

(5) Subject to paragraph (4), county court rules may—

(a) apply any of the provisions of Part I of the Arbitration Act 1996 to arbitrations under paragraph (3) with such modifications as may be prescribed;

(b) prescribe the rules of evidence to be followed on any arbitration under paragraph (3) and, in particular, make provision with respect to the manner of taking and questioning evidence.

(5A) Except as provided by virtue of paragraph (5)(a), Part I of the Arbitration Act 1996 shall not apply to an arbitration under paragraph (3).".

(3) After Article 61 insert—

"Appeals from decisions under Part I of Arbitration Act 1996

61A.—(1) Article 61 does not apply to a decision of a county court judge made in the exercise of the jurisdiction conferred by Part I of the Arbitration Act 1996.
(2) Any party dissatisfied with a decision of the county court made in the exercise of the jurisdiction conferred by any of the following provisions of Part I of the Arbitration Act 1996, namely—

(a) section 32 (question as to substantive jurisdiction of arbitral tribunal);

(b) section 45 (question of law arising in course of arbitral proceedings);

(c) section 67 (challenging award of arbitral tribunal: substantive jurisdiction);

(d) section 68 (challenging award of arbitral tribunal: serious irregularity);

(e) section 69 (appeal on point of law),

may, subject to the provisions of that Part, appeal from that decision to the Court of Appeal.
(3) Any party dissatisfied with any decision of a county court made in the exercise of the jurisdiction conferred by any other provision of Part I of the Arbitration Act 1996 may, subject to the provisions of that Part, appeal from that decision to the High Court.
(4) The decision of the Court of Appeal on an appeal under paragraph (2) shall be final.".

Supreme Court Act 1981 (c.54)

37.—(1) The Supreme Court Act 1981 is amended as follows.
(2) In section 18(1) (restrictions on appeals to the Court of Appeal), for paragraph (g) substitute—

"(g) except as provided by Part I of the Arbitration Act 1996, from any decision of the High Court under that Part;".

(3) In section 151 (interpretation, &c.), in the definition of "arbitration agreement", for "the Arbitration Act 1950 by virtue of section 32 of that Act;" substitute "Part I of the Arbitration Act 1996;".

Merchant Shipping (Liner Conferences) Act 1982 (c.37)

38.—In section 7(5) of the Merchant Shipping (Liner Conferences) Act 1982 (stay of legal proceedings), for the words from "section 4(1)" to the end substitute "section 9 of the Arbitration Act 1996 (which also provides for the staying of legal proceedings).".

Agricultural Marketing (Northern Ireland) Order 1982 (N.I.12)

39.—In Article 14 of the Agricultural Marketing (Northern Ireland) Order 1982 (application of provisions of Arbitration Act (Northern Ireland) 1937)—

(a) for the words from the beginning to "shall apply" substitute "Section 45 and 69 of the Arbitration Act 1996 (which relate to the determination by the court of questions of law) and section 66 of that Act (enforcement of awards)" apply; and

(b) for "an arbitration" substitute "arbitral proceedings".

Mental Health Act 1983 (c.20)

40.—In section 78 of the Mental Health Act 1983 (procedure of Mental Health Review Tribunals), in subsection (9) for "The Arbitration Act 1950" substitute "Part I of the Arbitration Act 1996".

Registered Homes Act 1984 (c.23)

41.—In section 43 of the Registered Homes Act 1984 (procedure of Registered Homes Tribunals), in subsection (3) for "The Arbitration Act 1950" substitute "Part I of the Arbitration Act 1996".

Housing Act 1985 (c.68)

42.—In section 47(3) of the Housing Act 1985 (agreement as to determination of matters relating to service charges) for "section 32 of the Arbitration Act 1950" substitute "Part I of the Arbitration Act 1996".

Landlord and Tenant Act 1985 (c.70)

43.—In section 19(3) of the Landlord and Tenant Act 1985 (agreement as to determination of matters relating to service charges), for "section 32 of the Arbitration Act 1950" substitute "Part I of the Arbitration Act 1996".

Credit Unions (Northern Ireland) Order 1985 (N.I.12)

44.—(1) Article 72 of the Credit Unions (Northern Ireland) Order 1985 (decision of disputes) is amended as follows.

(2) In paragraph (7)—

(a) in the opening words, omit the words from "and without prejudice" to "1937";

(b) at the beginning of sub-paragraph (a) insert "without prejudice to any powers exercisable by virtue of Part I of the Arbitration Act 1996,"; and

(c) in sub-paragraph (b) omit "the registrar or" and "registrar or" and for the words from "as might have been granted by the High Court" to the end substitute "as might be granted by the registrar".

(3) For paragraph (8) substitute—

"(8) The court or registrar to whom any dispute is referred under paragraphs (2) to (6) may at the request of either party state a case on any question of law arising in the dispute for the opinion of the High Court.".

Agricultural Holdings Act 1986 (c.5)

45.—In section 84(1) of the Agricultural Holdings Act 1986 (provisions relating to arbitration), for "the Arbitration Act 1950" substitute "Part I of the Arbitration Act 1996".

Insolvency Act 1986 (c.45)

46.—In the Insolvency Act 1986, after section 349 insert—
"Arbitration agreements to which bankrupt is party.
349A.—(1) This section applies where a bankrupt had become party to a contract containing an arbitration agreement before the commencement of his bankruptcy.
(2) If the trustee in bankruptcy adopts the contract, the arbitration agreement is enforceable by or against the trustee in relation to matters arising from or connected with the contract.
(3) If the trustee in bankruptcy does not adopt the contract and a matter to which the arbitration agreement applies requires to be determined in connection with or for the purposes of the bankruptcy proceedings—

(a) the trustee with the consent of the creditors' committee, or

(b) any other party to the agreement,

may apply to the court which may, if it thinks fit in all the circumstances of the case, order that the matter be referred to arbitration in accordance with the arbitration agreement.
(4) In this section—
"arbitration agreement" has the same meaning as in Part I of the Arbitration Act 1996; and

"the court" means the court which has jurisdiction in the bankruptcy proceedings.".

Building Societies Act 1986 (c.53)

47.—In Part II of Schedule 14 to the Building Societies Act 1986 (settlement of disputes: arbitration), in paragraph 5(6) for "the Arbitration Act 1950 and the Arbitration Act 1979 or, in Northern Ireland, the Arbitration Act (Northern Ireland) 1937" substitute "Part I of the Arbitration Act 1996".

Mental Health (Northern Ireland) Order 1986 (N.I.4)

48.—In Article 83 of the Mental Health (Northern Ireland) Order 1986 (procedure of Mental Health Review Tribunal), in paragraph (8) for "The Arbitration Act (Northern Ireland) 1937" substitute "Part I of the Arbitration Act 1996".

Multilateral Investment Guarantee Agency Act 1988 (c.8)

49.—For section 6 of the Multilateral Investment Guarantee Agency Act 1988 (application of Arbitration Act) substitute—

"Application of Arbitration Act.

6.—(1) The Lord Chancellor may by order made by statutory instrument direct that any of the provisions of sections 36 and 38 to 44 of the Arbitration Act 1996 (provisions in relation to the conduct of the arbitral proceedings, &c.) apply, with such modifications or exceptions as are specified in the order, to such arbitration proceedings pursuant to Annex II to the Convention as are specified in the order.

(2) Except as provided by an order under subsection (1) above, no provision of Part I of the Arbitration Act 1996 other than section 9 (stay of legal proceedings) applies to any such proceedings.".

Copyright, Designs and Patents Act 1988 (c.48)

50.—In section 150 of the Copyright, Designs and Patents Act 1988 (Lord Chancellor's power to make rules for Copyright Tribunal), for subsection (2) substitute—

"(2) The rules may apply in relation to the Tribunal, as respects proceedings in England and Wales or Northern Ireland, any of the provisions of Part I of the Arbitration Act 1996.".

Fair Employment (Northern Ireland) Act 1989 (c.32)

51.—In the Fair Employment (Northern Ireland) Act 1989, section 5(7) (procedure of Fair Employment Tribunal), for "The Arbitration Act (Northern Ireland) 1937" substitute "Part I of the Arbitration Act 1996".

Limitation (Northern Ireland) Order 1989 (N.I.11)

52.—In Article 2(2) of the Limitation (Northern Ireland) Order 1989 (interpretation), in the definition of "arbitration agreement", for "the Arbitration Act (Northern Ireland) 1937" substitute "Part I of the Arbitration Act 1996".

Insolvency (Northern Ireland) Order 1989 (N.I.19)

53.—In the Insolvency (Northern Ireland) Order 1989, after Article 320 insert—

"Arbitration agreements to which bankrupt is party.

320A.—(1) This Article applies where a bankrupt had become party to a contract containing an arbitration agreement before the commencement of his bankruptcy.
(2) If the trustee in bankruptcy adopts the contract, the arbitration agreement is enforceable by or against the trustee in relation to matters arising from or connected with the contract.
(3) If the trustee in bankruptcy does not adopt the contract and a matter to which the arbitration agreement applies requires to be determined in connection with or for the purposes of the bankruptcy proceedings—

(a) the trustee with the consent of the creditors' committee, or

(b) any other party to the agreement,

may apply to the court which may, if it thinks fit in all the circumstances of the case, order that the matter be referred to arbitration in accordance with the arbitration agreement.
(4) In this Article—
'arbitration agreement' has the same meaning as in Part I of the Arbitration Act 1996; and
'the court' means the court which has jurisdiction in the bankruptcy proceedings.".

Social Security Administration Act 1992 (c.5)

54.—In section 59 of the Social Security Administration Act 1992 (procedure for inquiries, &c.), in subsection (7), for "The Arbitration Act 1950" substitute "Part I of the Arbitration Act 1996".

Social Security Administration (Northern Ireland) Act 1992 (c.8)

55.—In section 57 of the Social Security Administration (Northern Ireland) Act 1992 (procedure for inquiries, &c.), in subsection (6) for "the

Arbitration Act (Northern Ireland) 1937" substitute "Part I of the Arbitration Act 1996".

Trade Union and Labour Relations (Consolidation) Act 1992 (c.52)

56.—In sections 212(5) and 263(6) of the Trade Union and Labour Relations (Consolidation) Act 1992 (application of Arbitration Act) for "the Arbitration Act 1950" substitute "Part I of the Arbitration Act 1996".

Industrial Relations (Northern Ireland) Order 1992 (N.I.5)

57.—In Articles 84(9) and 92(5) of the Industrial Relations (Northern Ireland) Order 1992 (application of Arbitration Act) for "The Arbitration Act (Northern Ireland) 1937" substitute "Part I of the Arbitration Act 1996".

Registered Homes (Northern Ireland) Order 1992 (N.I.20)

58.—In Article 33(3) of the Registered Homes (Northern Ireland) Order 1992 (procedure of Registered Homes Tribunal) for "The Arbitration Act (Northern Ireland) 1937" substitute "Part I of the Arbitration Act 1996".

Education Act 1993 (c.35)

59.—In section 180(4) of the Education Act 1993 (procedure of Special Educational Needs Tribunal), for "The Arbitration Act 1950" substitute "Part I of the Arbitration Act 1996".

Roads (Northern Ireland) Order 1993 (N.I.15)

60.—(1) The Roads (Northern Ireland) Order 1993 is amended as follows.
(2) In Article 131 (application of Arbitration Act) for "the Arbitration Act (Northern Ireland) 1937" substitute "Part I of the Arbitration Act 1996".
(3) In Schedule 4 (disputes), in paragraph 3(2) for "the Arbitration Act (Northern Ireland) 1937" substitute "Part I of the Arbitration Act 1996".

Merchant Shipping Act 1995 (c.21)

61.—In Part II of Schedule 6 to the Merchant Shipping Act 1995 (provisions having effect in connection with Convention Relating to the Carriage of Passengers and Their Luggage by Sea), for paragraph 7 substitute—

> "**7.** Article 16 shall apply to arbitral proceedings as it applies to an action; and, as respects England and Wales and Northern Ireland, the provisions of section 14 of the Arbitration Act 1996 apply to determine for the purposes of that Article when an arbitration is commenced.".

Industrial Tribunals Act 1996 (c.17)

62.—In section 6(2) of the Industrial Tribunals Act 1996 (procedure of industrial tribunals), for "The Arbitration Act 1950" substitute "Part I of the Arbitration Act 1996".

SCHEDULE 4

Schedule 107(2)

Repeals

Chapter Short title
Extent of repeal

1892 c. 43.
Military Lands Act 1892.
In section 21(b), the words "under the Arbitration Act 1889".

1922 c. 51.
Allotments Act 1922.
In section 21(3), the words "under the Arbitration Act 1889".

1937 c. 8 (N.I.).
Arbitration Act (Northern Ireland) 1937.
The whole Act.

1949 c. 54.
Wireless Telegraphy Act 1949.
In Schedule 2, paragraph 3(3).

1949 c. 97.
National Parks and Access to the Countryside Act 1949.
In section 18(4), the words from "Without prejudice" to "England or Wales".

1950 c. 27.
Arbitration Act 1950.
Part I. Section 42(3).

1958 c. 47.
Agricultural Marketing Act 1958.
Section 53(8).

1962 c. 46.
Transport Act 1962.
In Schedule 11, Part II, paragraph 7.

1964 c. 14.
Plant Varieties and Seeds Act 1964.

In section 10(4) the words from "or in section 9" to "three arbitrators".
Section 39(3)(b)(i).

1964 c. 29 (N.I.).
Lands Tribunal and Compensation Act (Northern Ireland) 1964.
In section 9(3) the words from "so, however, that" to the end.

1965 c. 12.
Industrial and Provident Societies Act 1965.
In section 60(8)(b), the words "by virtue of section 12 of the said Act of 1950".

1965 c. 37.
Carriage of Goods by Road Act 1965.
Section 7(2)(b).

1965 c. 13 (N.I.).
New Towns Act (Northern Ireland) 1965.
In section 27(2), the words from "under and in accordance with" to the end.

1969 c. 24 (N.I.).
Industrial and Provident Societies Act (Northern Ireland) 1969.
In section 69(7)—
(a) in the opening words, the words from "and without prejudice" to "1937";
(b) in paragraph (b), the words "the registrar or" and "registrar or".

1970 c. 31.
Administration of Justice Act 1970.
Section 4.
Schedule 3.

1973 c. 41.
Fair Trading Act 1973.
Section 33(2)(d).

1973 N.I. 1.
Drainage (Northern Ireland) Order 1973.
In Article 15(4), the words from "under and in accordance" to the end.
Article 40(4).

In Schedule 7, in paragraph 9(2), the words from "under and in accordance" to the end.

1974 c. 47.
Solicitors Act 1974.
In section 87(1), in the definition of "contentious business", the words "appointed under the Arbitration Act 1950".

1975 c. 3.
Arbitration Act 1975.
The whole Act.

1975 c. 74.
Petroleum and Submarine Pipe-Lines Act 1975.
In Part II of Schedule 2–
(a) in model clause 40(2), the words "in accordance with the Arbitration Act 1950";
(b) in model clause 40(2B), the words "in accordance with the Arbitration Act (Northern Ireland) 1937".
In Part II of Schedule 3, in model clause 38(2), the words "in accordance with the Arbitration Act 1950".

1976 N.I. 12.
Solicitors (Northern Ireland) Order 1976.
In Article 3(2), in the entry "contentious business", the words "appointed under the Arbitration Act (Northern Ireland) 1937".
Article 71H(3).

1977 c. 37.
Patents Act 1977.
In section 52(4) the words "section 21 of the Arbitration Act 1950 or, as the case may be, section 22 of the Arbitration Act (Northern Ireland) 1937 (statement of cases by arbitrators); but".
Section 131(e).

1977 c. 38.
Administration of Justice Act 1977.
Section 17(2).

1978 c. 23.
Judicature (Northern Ireland) Act 1978.
In section 35(2), paragraph (g)(v).
In Schedule 5, the amendment to the Arbitration Act 1950.

1979 c. 42.
Arbitration Act 1979.
The whole Act.

1980 c. 58.
Limitation Act 1980.
Section 34.

1980 N.I. 3.
County Courts (Northern Ireland) Order 1980.
Article 31(3).

1981 c. 54.
Supreme Court Act 1981.
Section 148.

1982 c. 27.
Civil Jurisdiction and Judgments Act 1982.
Section 25(3)(c) and (5).
In section 26–
(a) in subsection (1), the words "to arbitration or";
(b) in subsection (1)(a)(i), the words "arbitration or";
(c) in subsection (2), the words "arbitration or".

1982 c. 53.
Administration of Justice Act 1982.
Section 15(6).
In Schedule 1, Part IV.

1984 c. 5.
Merchant Shipping Act 1984.
Section 4(8).

1984 c. 12.
Telecommunications Act 1984.
Schedule 2, paragraph 13(8).

1984 c. 16.
Foreign Limitation Periods Act 1984.
Section 5.

1984 c. 28.
County Courts Act 1984.
In Schedule 2, paragraph 70.

1985 c. 61.
Administration of Justice Act 1985.
Section 58.
In Schedule 9, paragraph 15.

1985 c. 68.
Housing Act 1985.
In Schedule 18, in paragraph 6(2) the words from "and the Arbitration Act 1950" to the end.

1985 N.I. 12.
Credit Unions (Northern Ireland) Order 1985.
In Article 72(7)—
(a) in the opening words, the words from "and without prejudice" to"1937";
(b) in sub-paragraph (b), the words "the registrar or" and "registrar or".

1986 c. 45.
In Schedule 14, the entry relating to the Arbitration Act 1950.

1988 c. 8.
Section 8(3).

1988 c. 21.
The whole Act.

1989 N.I. 11.
Article 72.
In Schedule 3, paragraph 1.

1989 N.I. 19.
In Part II of Schedule 9, paragraph 66.

1990 c. 41.
Sections 99 and 101 to 103.

1991 N.I. 7.
In Articles 8(8) and 11(10), the words from "and the provisions" to the end.

1992 c. 40.
In Schedule 16, paragraph 30(1).

1995 c. 8.
Section 28(4).

1995 c. 21.
Section 96(10).
Section 264(9).

1995 c. 42.
Section 3.

APPENDIX 2

THE ARBITRATION ACT 1996 (COMMENCEMENT NO.1) ORDER 1996

(S.I. 1996 No. 3146)

Made .... *16th December 1996*

The Secretary of State, in exercise of the powers conferred on him by section 109 ot the Arbitration Act 1996(a), hereby makes the following Order:

1.—This Order may be cited as the Arbitration Act 1996 (Commencement No.1) Order 1996.

2.—The provisions of the Arbitration Act 1996 ("the Act") listed in Schedule 1 to this Order shall come into force on the day after this Order is made.

3.—The rest of the Act, except sections 85 to 87, shall come into force on 31st January, 1997.

4.—The transitional provisions in Schedule 2 to this Order shall have effect.

John M Taylor,
Parliamentary Under-Secretary of State
for Corporate and Consumer Affairs,
16th December, 1996 Department of Trade and Industry

SCHEDULE 1

Article 2.

Section 91 so far as it relates to the power to make orders under the section.

Section 105.

Section 107(1) and paragraph 36 of Schedule 3, so far as relating to the provision that may be made by county court rules.

Section 107(2) and the reference in Schedule 4 to the County Courts (Northern Ireland) Order 1980 so far as relating to the above matter.

Sections 108 to 110.

SCHEDULE 2

Article 4.

1.—In this Schedule:

(a) "the appointed day" means the date specified in Article 3 of this Order;

(b) "arbitration application" means any application relating to arbitration made by or in legal proceedings, whether or not arbitral proceedings have commenced;

(c) "the old law" means the enactments specified in section 107 as they stood before their amendment or repeal by the Act.

2.—The old law shall continue to apply to:

(a) arbitral proceedings commenced before the appointed day;

(b) arbitration applications commenced or made before the appointed day;

(c) arbitration applications commenced or made on or after the appointed day relating to arbitrial proceedings commenced before the appointed day,

and the provisions of the Act which would otherwise be applicable shall apply.

3.—The provisions of this Act brought into force by this Order shall apply to any other arbitration application.

4.—In the application of paragraph (b) of subsection (1) of section 46 (provision for dispute tobe decided in accordance with provisions other than law) to an arbitration agreement made before the appointed day, the agreement shall have effect in accordance with the rules of law (including any conflict of laws rules) as they stood immediately before the appointed day.

APPENDIX 3

THE UNFAIR TERMS IN CONSUMER CONTRACTS REGULATIONS 1999

(S.I. 1999 No. 2083)

Made ....*22nd July 1999*
Laid before Parliament ....*22nd July 1999*
Coming into force ....*1st October 1999*

Whereas the Secretary of State is a Minister designated for the purposes of section 2(2) of the European Communities Act 1972 in relation to measures relating to consumer protection:

Now, the Secretary of State, in exercise of the powers conferred upon him by section 2(2) of that Act, hereby makes the following Regulations.—

Citation and commencement

1.—These Regulations may be cited as the Unfair Terms in Consumer Contracts Regulations 1999 and shall come into force on 1st October 1999.

Revocation

2.—The Unfair Terms in Consumer Contracts Regulations 1994 are hereby revoked.

Interpretation

3.—(1) In these Regulations—

"the Community" means the European Community;

"consumer" means any natural person who, in contracts covered by these Regulations, is acting for purposes which are outside his trade, business or profession;

"court" in relation to England and Wales and Northern Ireland means a county court or the High Court, and in relation to Scotland, the Sheriff or the Court of Session;

"Director" means the Director General of Fair Trading;

"EEA Agreement" means the Agreement on the European Economic Area signed at Oporto on 2nd May 1992 as adjusted by the protocol signed at Brussels on 17th March 1993;

"Member State" means a State which is a contracting party to the EEA Agreement;

"notified" means notified in writing;

"qualifying body" means a person specified in Schedule 1;

"seller or supplier" means any natural or legal person who, in contracts covered by these Regulations, is acting for purposes relating to his trade, business or profession, whether publicly owned or privately owned;

"unfair terms" means the contractual terms referred to in regulation 5.

(2) In the application of these Regulations to Scotland for references to an "injunction" or an "interim injunction" there shall be substituted references to an "interdict" or "interim interdict" respectively.

Terms to which these Regulations apply

4.—(1) These Regulations apply in relation to unfair terms in contracts concluded between a seller or a supplier and a consumer.
(2) These Regulations do not apply to contractual terms which reflect—

(a) mandatory statutory or regulatory provisions (including such provisions under the law of any Member State or in Community legislation having effect in the United Kingdom without further enactment);

(b) the provisions or principles of international conventions to which the Member States or the Community are party.

Unfair Terms

5.—(1) A contractual term which has not been individually negotiated shall be regarded as unfair if, contrary to the requirement of good faith, it causes a significant imbalance in the parties' rights and obligations arising under the contract, to the detriment of the consumer.
(2) A term shall always be regarded as not having been individually negotiated where it has been drafted in advance and the consumer has therefore not been able to influence the substance of the term.
(3) Notwithstanding that a specific term or certain aspects of it in a contract has been individually negotiated, these Regulations shall apply to the rest of a contract if an overall assessment of it indicates that it is a pre-formulated standard contract.
(4) It shall be for any seller or supplier who claims that a term was individually negotiated to show that it was.
(5) Schedule 2 to these Regulations contains an indicative and non-exhaustive list of the terms which may be regarded as unfair.

Assessment of unfair terms

6.—(1) Without prejudice to regulation 12, the unfairness of a contractual term shall be assessed, taking into account the nature of the goods or services for which the contract was concluded and by referring, at the time of conclusion of the contract, to all the circumstances attending the conclusion of the contract and to all the other terms of the contract or of another contract on which it is dependent.
(2) In so far as it is in plain intelligible language, the assessment of fairness of a term shall not relate—

(a) to the definition of the main subject matter of the contract, or

(b) to the adequacy of the price or remuneration, as against the goods or services supplied in exchange.

Written contracts

7.—(1) A seller or supplier shall ensure that any written term of a contract is expressed in plain, intelligible language.
(2) If there is doubt about the meaning of a written term, the interpretation which is most favourable to the consumer shall prevail but this rule shall not apply in proceedings brought under regulation 12.

Effect of unfair term

8.—(1) An unfair term in a contract concluded with a consumer by a seller or supplier shall not be binding on the consumer.
(2) The contract shall continue to bind the parties if it is capable of continuing in existence without the unfair term.

Choice of law clauses

9.—These Regulations shall apply notwithstanding any contract term which applies or purports to apply the law of a non-Member State, if the contract has a close connection with the territory of the Member States.

Complaints—consideration by Director

10.—(1) It shall be the duty of the Director to consider any complaint made to him that any contract term drawn up for general use is unfair, unless—

(a) the complaint appears to the Director to be frivolous or vexatious; or

(b) a qualifying body has notified the Director that it agrees to consider the complaint.

(2) The Director shall give reasons for his decision to apply or not to apply, as the case may be, for an injunction under regulation 12 in relation to any complaint which these Regulations require him to consider.

(3) In deciding whether or not to apply for an injunction in respect of a term which the Director considers to be unfair, he may, if he considers it appropriate to do so, have regard to any undertakings given to him by or on behalf of any person as to the continued use of such a term in contracts concluded with consumers.

Complaints—consideration by qualifying bodies

11.—(1) If a qualifying body specified in Part One of Schedule 1 notifies the Director that it agrees to consider a complaint that any contract term drawn up for general use is unfair, it shall be under a duty to consider that complaint.
(2) Regulation 10(2) and (3) shall apply to a qualifying body which is under a duty to consider a complaint as they apply to the Director.

Injunctions to prevent continued use of unfair terms

12.—(1) The Director or, subject to paragraph (2), any qualifying body may apply for an injunction (including an interim injunction) against any person appearing to the Director or that body to be using, or recommending use of, an unfair term drawn up for general use in contracts concluded with consumers.
(2) A qualifying body may apply for an injunction only where-

(a) it has notified the Director of its intention to apply at least fourteen days before the date on which the application is made, beginning with the date on which the notification was given; or

(b) the Director consents to the application being made within a shorter period.

(3) The court on an application under this regulation may grant an injunction on such terms as it thinks fit.
(4) An injunction may relate not only to use of a particular contract term drawn up for general use but to any similar term, or a term having like effect, used or recommended for use by any person.

Powers of the Director and qualifying bodies to obtain documents and information

13.—(1) The Director may exercise the power conferred by this regulation for the purpose of—

(a) facilitating his consideration of a complaint that a contract term drawn up for general use is unfair; or

(b) ascertaining whether a person has complied with an undertaking or court order as to the continued use, or recommendation for use, of a term in contracts concluded with consumers.

(2) A qualifying body specified in Part One of Schedule 1 may exercise the power conferred by this regulation for the purpose of—

(a) facilitating its consideration of a complaint that a contract term drawn up for general use is unfair; or

(b) ascertaining whether a person has complied with—

(i) an undertaking given to it or to the court following an application by that body, or

(ii) a court order made on an application by that body,

as to the continued use, or recommendation for use, of a term in contracts concluded with consumers.

(3) The Director may require any person to supply to him, and a qualifying body specified in Part One of Schedule 1 may require any person to supply to it—

(a) a copy of any document which that person has used or recommended for use, at the time the notice referred to in paragraph (4) below is given, as a pre-formulated standard contract in dealings with consumers;

(b) information about the use, or recommendation for use, by that person of that document or any other such document in dealings with consumers.

(4) The power conferred by this regulation is to be exercised by a notice in writing which may—

(a) specify the way in which and the time within which it is to be complied with; and

(b) be varied or revoked by a subsequent notice.

(5) Nothing in this regulation compels a person to supply any document or information which he would be entitled to refuse to produce or give in civil proceedings before the court.

(6) If a person makes default in complying with a notice under this regulation, the court may, on the application of the Director or of the qualifying body, make such order as the court thinks fit for requiring the default to be made good, and any such order may provide that all the costs or expenses of and incidental to the application shall be borne by the person in default or by any officers of a company or other association who are responsible for its default.

Notification of undertakings and orders to Director

14.—A qualifying body shall notify the Director—

(a) of any undertaking given to it by or on behalf of any person as to the continued use of a term which that body considers to be unfair in contracts concluded with consumers;

(b) of the outcome of any application made by it under regulation 12, and of the terms of any undertaking given to, or order made by, the court;

(c) of the outcome of any application made by it to enforce a previous order of the court.

Publication, information and advice

15.—(1) The Director shall arrange for the publication in such form and manner as he considers appropriate, of—

(a) details of any undertaking or order notified to him under regulation 14;

(b) details of any undertaking given to him by or on behalf of any person as to the continued use of a term which the Director considers to be unfair in contracts concluded with consumers;

(c) details of any application made by him under regulation 12, and of the terms of any undertaking given to, or order made by, the court;

(d) details of any application made by the Director to enforce a previous order of the court.

(2) The Director shall inform any person on request whether a particular term to which these Regulations apply has been—

(a) the subject of an undertaking given to the Director or notified to him by a qualifying body; or

(b) the subject of an order of the court made upon application by him or notified to him by a qualifying body;

and shall give that person details of the undertaking or a copy of the order, as the case may be, together with a copy of any amendments which the person giving the undertaking has agreed to make to the term in question.

(3) The Director may arrange for the dissemination in such form and manner as he considers appropriate of such information and advice concerning the operation of these Regulations as may appear to him to be expedient to give to the public and to all persons likely to be affected by these Regulations.

Kim Howells
Parliamentary Under-Secretary of State for Competition and Consumer Affairs, Department of Trade and Industry.

22nd July 1999

SCHEDULE 1

Regulation 3

Qualifying Bodies

Part One

1. The Data Protection Registrar.
2. The Director General of Electricity Supply.
3. The Director General of Gas Supply.
4. The Director General of Electricity Supply for Northern Ireland.
5. The Director General of Gas for Northern Ireland.
6. The Director General of Telecommunications.
7. The Director General of Water Services.
8. The Rail Regulator.
9. Every weights and measures authority in Great Britain.
10. The Department of Economic Development in Northern Ireland.

Part Two

11. Consumers' Association.

SCHEDULE 2

Regulation 5(5)

Indicative and Non-Exhaustive List of Terms Which May be Regarded as Unfair

1. Terms which have the object or effect of-

(a) excluding or limiting the legal liability of a seller or supplier in the event of the death of a consumer or personal injury to the latter resulting from an act or omission of that seller or supplier;

(b) inappropriately excluding or limiting the legal rights of the consumer vis-à-vis the seller or supplier or another party in the event of total or partial non-performance or inadequate performance by the seller or supplier of any of the contractual obligations, including the option of offsetting a debt owed to the seller or supplier against any claim which the consumer may have against him;

(c) making an agreement binding on the consumer whereas provision of services by the seller or supplier is subject to a condition whose realisation depends on his own will alone;

(d) permitting the seller or supplier to retain sums paid by the consumer where the latter decides not to conclude or perform the contract, without providing for the consumer to receive compensation of an equivalent amount from the seller or supplier where the latter is the party cancelling the contract;

(e) requiring any consumer who fails to fulfil his obligation to pay a disproportionately high sum in compensation;

(f) authorising the seller or supplier to dissolve the contract on a discretionary basis where the same facility is not granted to the consumer, or permitting the seller or supplier to retain the sums paid for services not yet supplied by him where it is the seller or supplier himself who dissolves the contract;

(g) enabling the seller or supplier to terminate a contract of indeterminate duration without reasonable notice except where there are serious grounds for doing so;

(h) automatically extending a contract of fixed duration where the consumer does not indicate otherwise, when the deadline fixed for the consumer to express his desire not to extend the contract is unreasonably early;

(i) irrevocably binding the consumer to terms with which he had no real opportunity of becoming acquainted before the conclusion of the contract;

(j) enabling the seller or supplier to alter the terms of the contract unilaterally without a valid reason which is specified in the contract;

(k) enabling the seller or supplier to alter unilaterally without a valid reason any characteristics of the product or service to be provided;

(l) providing for the price of goods to be determined at the time of delivery or allowing a seller of goods or supplier of services to increase their price without in both cases giving the consumer the corresponding right to cancel the contract if the final price is too high in relation to the price agreed when the contract was concluded;

(m) giving the seller or supplier the right to determine whether the goods or services supplied are in conformity with the contract, or giving him the exclusive right to interpret any term of the contract;

(n) limiting the seller's or supplier's obligation to respect commitments undertaken by his agents or making his commitments subject to compliance with a particular formality;

(o) obliging the consumer to fulfil all his obligations where the seller or supplier does not perform his;

(p) giving the seller or supplier the possibility of transferring his rights and obligations under the contract, where this may serve to reduce the guarantees for the consumer, without the latter's agreement;

(q) excluding or hindering the consumer's right to take legal action or exercise any other legal remedy, particularly by requiring the consumer to take disputes exclusively to arbitration not covered by legal provisions, unduly restricting the evidence available to him or imposing on him a burden of proof which, according to the applicable law, should lie with another party to the contract.

2. Scope of paragraphs 1(g), (j) and (l)

(a) Paragraph 1(g) is without hindrance to terms by which a supplier of financial services reserves the right to terminate unilaterally a contract of indeterminate duration without notice where there is a valid reason, provided that the supplier is required to inform the other contracting party or parties thereof immediately.

(b) Paragraph 1(j) is without hindrance to terms under which a supplier of financial services reserves the right to alter the rate of interest payable by the consumer or due to the latter, or the amount of other charges for financial services without notice where there is a valid reason, provided that the supplier is required to inform the other contracting party or parties thereof at the earliest opportunity and that the latter are free to dissolve the contract immediately.

Paragraph 1(j) is also without hindrance to terms under which a seller or supplier reserves the right to alter unilaterally the conditions of a contract of indeterminate duration, provided that he is required to inform the consumer with reasonable notice and that the consumer is free to dissolve the contract.

(c) Paragraphs 1(g), (j) and (l) do not apply to:

—transactions in transferable securities, financial instruments and other products or services where the price is linked to fluctuations in a stock exchange quotation or index or a financial market rate that the seller or supplier does not control;—contracts for the purchase or sale of foreign currency, traveller's cheques or international money orders denominated in foreign currency;

(d) Paragraph 1(l) is without hindrance to price indexation clauses, where lawful, provided that the method by which prices vary is explicitly described.

EXPLANATORY NOTE

(*This note is not part of the Regulations*)

These Regulations revoke and replace the Unfair Terms in Consumer Contracts Regulations 1994 (S.I. 1994/3159) which came into force on 1st July 1995.

Those Regulations implemented Council Directive 93/13/EEC on unfair terms in consumer contracts (O.J. No. L95, 21.4.93, p. 29). Regulations 3 to 9 of these Regulations re-enact regulations 2 to 7 of the 1994 Regulations with modifications to reflect more closely the wording of the Directive.

The Regulations apply, with certain exceptions, to unfair terms in contracts concluded between a consumer and a seller or supplier (regulation 4). The Regulations provide that an unfair term is one which has not been individually negotiated and which, contrary to the requirement of good faith, causes a significant imbalance in the parties' rights and obligations under the contract to the detriment of the consumer (regulation 5). Schedule 2 contains an indicative list of terms which may be regarded as unfair.

The assessment of unfairness will take into account all the circumstances attending the conclusion of the contract. However, the assessment is not to relate to the definition of the main subject matter of the contract or the adequacy of the price or remuneration as against the goods or services supplied in exchange as long as the terms concerned are in plain, intelligible language (regulation 6). Unfair contract terms are not binding on the consumer (regulation 8).

The Regulations maintain the obligation on the Director General of Fair Trading (contained in the 1994 Regulations) to consider any complaint made to him about the fairness of any contract term drawn up for general use. He may, if he considers it appropriate to do so, seek an injunction to prevent the continued use of that term or of a term having like effect (regulations 10 and 12).

The Regulations provide for the first time that a qualifying body named in Schedule 1 (statutory regulators, trading standards departments and Consumers' Association) may also apply for an injunction to prevent the continued use of an unfair contract term provided it has notified the Director General of its intention at least 14 days before the application is made (unless the Director General consents to a shorter period) (regulation 12). A qualifying body named in Part One of Schedule 1 (public bodies) shall be under a duty to consider a complaint if it has told the Director General that it will do so (regulation 11).

The Regulations provide a new power for the Director General and the public qualifying bodies to require traders to produce copies of their standard contracts, and give information about their use, in order to facilitate investigation of complaints and ensure compliance with undertakings or court orders (regulation 13).

Qualifying bodies must notify the Director General of undertakings given to them about the continued use of an unfair term and of the outcome of any court proceedings (regulation 14). The Director General is given the power to arrange for the publication of this information in such form and manner as he considers appropriate and to offer information and advice about the operation of these Regulations (regulation 15). In addition the Director General will supply enquirers about particular standard terms with details of any relevant undertakings and court orders.

A Regulatory Impact Assessment of the costs and benefits which will result from these Regulations has been prepared by the Department of Trade and Industry and is available from Consumer Affairs Directorate, Department of Trade and Industry, Room 407, 1 Victoria Street, London SW1H 0ET (Telephone 0171 215 0341). Copies have been placed in the libraries of both Houses of Parliament.

APPENDIX 4

ARBITRATION (SCOTLAND) ACT 1894

(57 & 58 Vict. c. 13)

An Act to amend the law of arbitration in scotland.

[3rd July 1894]

Reference to arbiter not named, etc., not to be invalid

1.—An agreement to refer to arbitration shall not be invalid or ineffectual by reason of the reference being to a person not named, or to a person to be named by another person, or to a person merely described as the holder for the time being of any office or appointment.

On failure to concur in nomination of single arbiter, court may appoint

2.—Should one of the parties to an agreement to refer to a single arbiter refuse to concur in the nomination of such arbiter, and should no provision have been made for carrying out the reference in that event, or should such provision have failed, an arbiter may be appointed by the court, on the application of any party to the agreement, and the arbiter so appointed shall have the same powers as if he had been duly nominated by all the parties.

On failure of one party to nominate arbiter, court may appoint

3.—Should one of the parties to an agreement to refer to two arbiters refuse to name an arbiter, in terms of the agreement, and should no provision have been made for carrying out the reference in that event, or should such provisions have failed, an arbiter may be appointed by the court, on the application of the other party, and the arbiter so appointed shall have the same powers as if he had been duly nominated by the party so refusing.

Arbiters may devolve on oversmen unless otherwise agreed

4.—Unless the agreement to refer shall otherwise provide, arbiters shall have power to name an oversmanon whom the reference shall be devolved in the event of their differing in opinion. Should the arbiters fail to agree in the nomination of an oversman, the court may on the application of any party to the agreement appoint an oversman. The decision of such oversman, whether he has been named by the arbiters or appointed by the court, shall be final.

Act not to apply to certain agreements

5.—This Act shall not apply to any agreement, made before its passing, to refer to an arbiter not named or to br named by another person or merely described as the holder for the time being of an office or appointment, if any party to such agreement shall, before the passing of this Act, or within six months thereafter, have intimated to the other party by writing that he declines to be bound by such agreement.

Interpretation

6.—For the purposes of this Act the expression "the court" shall mean any sheriff having jurisdiction or any Lord Ordinary of the Court of Session: except that where

(a) any arbiter appointed is; or

(b) in terms of the agreement to refer to arbitration an arbiter or oversman to be appointed must be, a Senator of the College of Justice, "the court" shall mean the Inner House of the Court of Session.

Extent of Act and short title

7.—This Act shall apply to Scotland only, and may be cited as the Arbitration (Scotland) Act 1894.

Appendix 5

ADMINISTRATION OF JUSTICE(SCOTLAND) ACT 1972

(1972 c. 59)

An Act to confer extended powers on the courts in Scotland to order the inspection of documents and other property, and related matters; to enable an appeal to be taken to the House of Lords from an intercutor of the Court of Session on a motion for a new trial; to enable a case to be stated on a question of law to the Court Session in an arbitration; and to enable alterations to be made by act of sederunt in the rate of interest to be included in sheriff court decrees or extracts. (9th August 1972)

Power of arbiter to state case to Court of Session

3.—(1) Subject to express provision to the contrary in an agreement to refer to arbitration, the arbiter or oversman may, on the application of a party to the arbitration, and shall, if the Court of Session on such an application so directs, at any stage in the arbitration state a case for the opinion of that Court on any question of law arising in the arbitration.

(2) This section shall not apply to an arbitration under any enactment which confers a power to appeal to or state a case for the opinion of a court tribunal in relation to that arbitration.

(3)[1] This section shall not apply to any form of arbitration relating to a trade dispute within the meaning of the Industrial Courts Act 1919 or relating to a trade dispute within the meaning of the Trade Union and Labour Relations Act 1974; to any other arbitration arising from a collective agreement within the meaning of the said Act of 1974; or to proceedings before the Industrial Arbitration Board.

(4) This section shall not apply in relation to an agreement to refer to arbitration made before the commencement of this Act.

[1] As amended by Trade Union and Labour Relations Act 1974, Sched. 3, para.17, Sched. 5.

5.—(1) This Act may be cited as the Administration of Justice (Scotland) Act 1972.

(2) In this Act any reference to an enactment shall be construed as a reference to that enactment as amended by or under any other enactment.

(3)[2] Sections 1 and 3 of this Act shall come into operation on such day as the Secretary of State may by order made by statutory instrument appoint, and different days may be appointed for different purposes.

(4) This Act shall extend to Scotland only.

[2] Power fully exercised: April 2, 1973, appointed for ss. 1 and 3 by S.I. 1973 No.339, art. 2.

INDEX